Praise for *Writing About Your Life*

"[Zinsser's] frank, affirmative and encouraging style will help anyone embarking on writing their own life story."
—PUBLISHERS WEEKLY

"Few people will be able to resist this cleverly designed memoir and course in memoir writing. It's not only elegantly written, but also touching, funny, wise and brimming with good advice. Another Zinsser classic."
—DIANE ACKERMAN, author of *A Natural History of the Senses*

"*Writing About Your Life* is not only a veritable treasure chest of good advice on writing a memoir—it is also rich in wisdom on how to live a creative life with integrity and courage. Like so many of William Zinsser's books, its deceptively simple style at first conceals but ultimately reveals a master craftsman—and a marvelously many-sided human being—in the midst of his journey."
—THOMAS FLEMING, novelist and historian

"This is a book of pure pleasure. You feel William Zinsser's enjoyment in finally joining his own stories with the other thing he loves: teaching. The reader goes right inside the writing process.
—NATALIE GOLDBERG, author of *Writing Down the Bones*

"If you are contemplating a memoir, I recommend William Zinsser's *Writing About Your Life* as an essential road map. Zinsser knows how to tell a good story, which makes tagging along with him on his wise and witty life's journey pure pleasure."
—ARTHUR GELB, editor and biographer

"It is difficult to imagine a better guide to writing compelling memoirs than William Zinsser. He is a writer's writer. . . . *Writing About Your Life* is autobiography as instruction. Readers will learn a great deal about Zinsser's absorbing years on earth while simultaneously absorbing lessons dropped into the text by the author. . . . This is a seamless memoir, the best kind. . . . Of all the lessons Zinsser shares, his emphasis on portraying memorable individuals memorably is almost certainly the most important. . . . Putting people into the manuscript is easy; choosing the right details about those people, choosing the right words to describe them, and—trickiest of all—choosing a unified point of view . . . well, those matters separate the published memoirist from the unpublished. . . . Reading this book means studying the master."
—THE WRITER

BOOKS IN PRINT

BY WILLIAM ZINSSER

On Writing Well HarperCollins

Writing to Learn HarperCollins

Mitchell & Ruff Paul Dry Books
(formerly *Willie and Dwike*)

Spring Training University of Pittsburgh Press

American Places The Akadine Press

*Easy to Remember: The Great American Songwriters
and Their Songs* David R. Godine, Publisher

Writing About Your Life Marlowe & Company

EDITED BY WILLIAM ZINSSER

Inventing the Truth: The Art and Craft of Memoir Houghton Mifflin

*Worlds of Childhood:
The Art and Craft of Writing for Children* Houghton Mifflin

Going on Faith: Writing as a Spiritual Quest Marlowe & Company

AUDIO BOOKS

BY WILLIAM ZINSSER

On Writing Well HarperCollins

Writing About Your Life

A Journey into the Past

William Zinsser

Da Capo
LIFE
LONG

A Member of the Perseus Books Group

Portions of this book first appeared in the *New York Times*, *Travel Holiday*, the *American Scholar*, the *Sewanee Review*, *Lingua Franca*, the *Atlantic Monthly* and in the books *Spring Training* and *Going on Faith*.

The passage by Russell Baker in chapter 10 and the passage by Ian Frazier in chapter 12 are from *Inventing the Truth: The Art and Craft of Memoir*, edited by William Zinsser (Houghton Mifflin, 1987, 1995, 1998). Copyright © 1987 by Russell Baker. Reprint by permission of Don Congdon Associates, Inc. Copyright © 1998 by Ian Frazier. Reprint by permission of the author.

The passage by Pablo Neruda in chapter 12 is an excerpt from *The Gift* by Lewis Hyde. Copyright © 1979, 1980, 1983 by W. Lewis Hyde. Used by permission of Random House, Inc.

Designed by Simon M. Sullivan
Set in 11 point ACaslon Regular by the Perseus Books Group

Cataloging-in-Publication data for this book is available from the Library of Congress.

ISBN: 978-1-56924-379-4

Published by Da Capo Press
A Member of the Perseus Books Group
www.dacapopress.com

Da Capo Press books are available at special discounts for bulk purchases in the U.S. by corporations, institutions, and other organizations. For more information, please contact the Special Markets Department at the Perseus Books Group, 2300 Chestnut Street, Suite 200, Philadelphia, PA, 19103, or call (800) 255-1514, or e-mail special.markets@perseusbooks.com.

CONTENTS

ACKNOWLEDGMENTS

I'm grateful to Matthew Lore, my editor and publisher, for his long and caring efforts to extract a memoir from me.

Once again I thank John S. Rosenberg, my onetime Yale student and longtime unofficial editor, for his many sensitive suggestions and improvements.

I also thank Al Silverman and Caroline Zinsser for their helpful reading of the manuscript.

Writing About Your Life

1.

Messages on My Machine

EVERY SO OFTEN I find on my answering machine in mid-Manhattan a brief cry for help. "What should be used to stop water stains coming through the ceiling?" the voice asks, or "Is it O.K. to use primer-sealer 1-2-3 for peeling paint in the bathroom?" I don't know anything about water stains and peeling paint; I'm a writer. The callers are trying to reach William Zinsser & Company, my father's shellac business. The company was in New York so long—well over a century—that some old customers think it's still there, and when they call directory assistance the number they're given is mine. I'm the only William Zinsser still doing business in New York; the firm moved away in 1975 and was later sold out of the family.

I don't mind getting the calls. Many of them are from hardware dealers in places like Moline and Winston-Salem and Fargo, and they remind me how much my father loved being an American businessman. But I also get calls from homeowners who are fixing up their homes and want product information. I call them all back to give them the right telephone number and to explain how they happened to get me. That's how I learned about Barbara Wallenstein and the trouble she was having with her picket fence in Newtown, Connecticut.

The William Zinsser who founded the business was my father's grandfather, who came from Germany in 1848 with a process for making shellac. He built a small house and factory far uptown in rural Manhattan, on what is now the block that runs from 58th and 59th Street on Tenth Avenue. I have a photograph of those two buildings standing alone in a rocky field that slopes down to the Hudson River. The only living creature is a goat. In its next generation the business did so poorly that it was near death when my father, the third William Zinsser, left college in 1909 to try to save it. His instincts as a merchant turned out to be sound, and he built the firm into the position it has occupied as the industry's leader ever since.

Quality was my father's passion. I never felt that he thought of his business as a means of making money, but as an art, to be practiced with only the best materials. Until he died at 91 his romance with shellac never faltered—my three older sisters and I knew at an early age the life cycle of the lac bug, which secretes a resinous cocoon onto the twigs of trees north of Calcutta—and he looked forward to the day when I would enter the firm. At that time the idea that a daughter could run a business as a well as a son—or better—was still a generation away.

But my romance was with a different business, and after I got home from World War II I got a job with the *New York Herald Tribune* and told my father I wouldn't be joining him. It was a painful moment for us both. Very few businesses stay in the same family in mid-Manhattan for more than 100 years, and the gods of continuity had hovered over my boyhood. My father accepted my decision with the generosity that was part of his character and wished me happiness in my chosen work. It was the best gift I ever received, freeing me to live my own life.

Deprived of one son, my father looked around for another and persuaded one of my sisters' husbands to come into the business, which thereby got a member of the family after all. Progress finally pushed the old company off its hillside. Roosevelt Hospital wanted the site for an expansion, and the shellac factory was a relic. Even in 1954, when my wife came into the family and was taken on a tour by my father, she could hardly believe that such a Dickensian agglomeration of pipes and vats still existed in industrial America. A modern plant was duly built in New Jersey in 1975 and the company left town. My father was then 87.

Only that move put an end to his walking to his office every day—a familiar white-haired figure in a Brooks Brothers suit and a bow tie and a Panama hat in summer, heading west on 59th Street, impatient to arrive, and not just to find out what orders had come in from Moline and Winston-Salem and Fargo. He was a lifelong citizen of New York, active on many boards that nourished its health and its cultural vigor: president of Lenox Hill Hospital, a member of the city's Art Commission and Landmarks Preservation Commission, an early raiser of funds to build Lincoln Center.

His insistence on the integrity of the product, whatever it was—shellac, hospital care, urban design, grand opera—came back to me one recent morning when I heard the beseeching voice of Mrs. Wallenstein on my answering machine. She was calling, she said, at 8:30 A.M. She had awakened with the resolve that this was the day when her picket fence was finally going to get painted. The weather was good and she was eager to start. She had a gallon of Zinsser's B-I-N and she needed to know if she could use it on the fence. Would I call back as soon as possible?

I got to my office around 10—writers' hours start later than shellac scions' hours—and called Mrs. Wallenstein. She was right by the phone. "I realized as soon as I got up today," she said, "that my husband is never going to paint that fence." I told her that although I was the son who didn't go into the business, she was calling about the one product I happened to know as a user, and I was sorry to have to tell her it should only be used indoors. She was no less sorry to hear it. I gave her the New Jersey phone number, explaining that the firm had been gone from West 59th Street for more than 15 years.

"I'm sure if you look at that can of B-I-N," I said, "the label gives the address as Somerset, New Jersey."

"I've got the can right here," she told me. "It says 516 West 59th Street."

4

"How long have you had that can, Mrs. Wallenstein?" I asked.

"Well, I guess we must have brought it with us when we moved from Long Island," she said.

We talked for a while about how "only yesterday" is always farther back than we think, and about how long it takes husbands to paint picket fences, and about fathers and sons and family businesses. Neither of us was in any hurry to get off the phone.

At the end Mrs. Wallenstein said, "It was very nice of you to call."

"My father would have wanted me to," I told her.

That article ran in the *New York Times* in 1991, and many people tell me they still remember it. They remember it because it deals with a number of universal themes: fathers and sons, family businesses, family expectations, filial duty, the continuity of cities, and several more. But I didn't set out to write about any of those themes. I just sat down one day to write a simple piece about an odd fact in my life as a writer: that I get messages on my answering machine from people who want to know how to spackle their bathroom. That's enough for one piece—an enjoyable and surprising subject. Every writer should get so lucky.

But as I started to write, all those other themes came tugging at my sleeve. And of course they belonged in my story. How could I write about the phone messages and not also talk about my father and his values as a businessman, and about his life as a New Yorker, and about his letting go of his dream for me and allowing me to follow my own dream. The act of writing told me what my piece was "about"—the many things it was about, including Mrs. Wallenstein, because the story isn't only about me and my father. It's also about my transaction with *her*.

Whatever we call the form—autobiography, memoir, personal history, family history—writing about one's life is a powerful human need. Who doesn't want to leave behind some record of his or her accomplishments and thoughts and emotions? If it's a family history it will have the further value of telling your children and your grandchildren who *they* are and what heritage *they* come from. Writers are the custodians of memory, and memories have a way of dying with their owner. One of the saddest sentences I know is "I wish I had asked my mother about that."

This book has two main premises. The first is: beware of "about." Beware of deciding in advance how your memoir or your family history will be organized and what it will say. Don't visualize the finished product at the end of your journey; it will look different when you get there. Be ready to be surprised by the crazy, wonderful events that will come dancing out of your past when you stir the pot of memory. Embrace those long-lost visitors. If they shove aside some events you originally thought you wanted to write about, it's because they have more vitality. Go with what interests and amuses you. Trust the process, and the product will take care of itself.

The other premise of the book is: think small. Notice how short my shellac article is: only a thousand words. Yet it tells you much of what you need to know about me and my family and my values. Remember this when you write about your own life. Don't rummage around in your past for "important" events—events you think are important enough to justify asking the rest of us to read about them. Write about small, self-contained incidents that are still vivid in your memory. If you remember them it's because they contain a larger truth that your readers will recognize in their own lives. Think small and you'll wind up finding the big themes in your family saga.

Whether your memoir ever gets published isn't finally the point. There are many good reasons for writing that have nothing to do with getting published. One is the personal satisfaction of coming to terms with your life narrative— getting your story sorted out and preserved on paper. Another is the archival satisfaction of leaving to your local library or historical society your memories of your community as you knew it when you were younger. This is priceless information for scholars and social historians. It doesn't have to take the form of a published book to give those scholars the facts they need. You can print your memoir handsomely on your computer and have it duplicated and bound by your local copy shop. The shelves of town and college libraries are rich in these homemade gems of recollection.

But you have a problem. There's a gap between wanting to write about your life and actually sitting down and doing it. The task looks overwhelming. How can you even begin to think about reducing the disorderly jumble of your past into a coherent narrative? How should you start? Where should you stop? What should you put in? What should you leave out? How should you organize the trip? Will you hurt anybody's feelings? Your head is full of memories longing to be written down. But your head is also full of doubts. Can you bring it off? And even if you do bring it off, will anybody care? Who gave you permission to think your story will interest the rest of us?

Well, *I* give you permission. All writers are embarked on a quest of some kind, and you're entitled to go on yours. My purpose in this book is to give you the permission and the tools. My method is to take you on a memoir of my own—to tell you about some people and places and events in my life that still amuse and often amaze me. Many of those events changed the direction of my career because I gave myself permission to not take the road I was expected to take, starting with not going into the family business that would have been a secure haven. Risk has been my ultimate safety net.

Along the way in these mini-memoirs I've paused to explain the technical decisions I made when I wrote them. They are the same kind of decisions you'll have to make when you write about *your* life. Mostly they are matters of craft: selection, reduction, organization, unity, voice, tone. But they are also matters of attitude: enjoyment, confidence, curiosity, intention, integrity, courage, grace. Those are the lubricants that keep us going and produce our best work. To write well about your life you only have to be true to yourself. If you make an honest transaction with your remembered experiences and emotions you'll reach the readers you want to reach.

This double journey into memoir—yours and mine—continues with one self-contained unit of time in my boyhood: four years spent in a small school in a New England village. But don't look for strict chronology or tidy connections in the rest of the trip. The journey itself will tell you—as it gradually told me—what the book is about.

2.

Writing About School

I SPENT FOUR YEARS AT a boys' boarding school in Massachusetts called Deerfield Academy. The years passed so uneventfully that I never wrote a memoir about them. I assumed that what happened during those years—the minutiae of everyday life—wouldn't interest anyone but me.

Part of the problem was that I was happy at Deerfield, and happy is bad news for writers. The only ones who can make a go of it are songwriters. Limited to 32 bars of music and armed with a vocabulary of simple words like "June" and "moon" that carry strong emotions, they can make us believe any romantic plot, no questions asked ("I took one look at you, that's all I meant to do, and then my heart stood still"). Nonfiction writers need sterner stuff, and many of them had the good luck—as writers—to be sent to schools that gave them plenty to be unhappy about. British writers were the luckiest of all. Their memoirs of the "public school" years are a cavalcade of sadistic masters and bullying upperclassmen, of caning and hazing and arcane sexual initiations. Anybody can write about *that*.

I'm also not an introspective writer; my interest is in people: what they do and what they say. During my four years at Deerfield—the volatile years of adolescence—I must have had my share of emotional growing pains. But they weren't so traumatic that I nursed them into adulthood and felt compelled to exorcise them in prose. Writers are stuck with the temperament they were born with, and I've always been glad to leave the interior life to its natural explorers.

So it was that my Deerfield days—and their strong influence on my life—went unrecorded. Then, one day in 1997, I got a call from the school. Various events were being planned to mark the bicentennial of the founding of the academy in 1797, including a commemorative book. It was to be a pictorial history, mostly photographs. But one memoir by an alumnus was also wanted. Would I write that memoir? I demurred. I pointed out that I could only speak for 4/200ths of the period the volume was supposed to cover—hardly a representative sample.

But the editor of the book kept asking me to "think about it," as editors will, and when I thought about it I realized that my years at Deerfield, far from being unrepresentative, fell at the very center of the modern history of the school. In 1902 a young man named Frank L. Boyden, just out of college, accepted a job that only a graduate desperate for employment might have taken: running an almost-defunct boys' academy in the tiny village of Deerfield. The school had so few students that the new headmaster had to play on the football and baseball teams himself. By the time I arrived, in 1936, Frank Boyden's school was just beginning to be recognized as one of the best in the country, and when he retired in 1968, his place in American education secure, he had been headmaster for 66 years. If I could write about the Boyden principles as I lived with them for four of those years, I would probably speak for all 66 years, because the principles never changed. I cranked my memory back, and these are the things I found myself remembering:

Of all the boarding schools I visited with my parents in 1936, Deerfield Academy was the only one I was willing to attend. Our tour began with some of the establishment schools in the Boston area that were founded on the English model and known for their tyrannical headmasters. That much-admired style was one I didn't happen to admire. A few summers earlier I had been sent to a proper boys' camp, run by an imperious Boston woman whose daily drill included fingernail inspection. No moment there went unfilled with worthy activity; we spent a lot of time braiding leather thongs and learning the Ojibway stroke. I wrote to my parents to come and get me, but they said they wouldn't think of it.

That rigid summer by the lake came back to me when we arrived at Milton Academy, the first stop on our school itinerary. It looked like a proper school, with red brick buildings and pristine playing fields, and the headmaster looked like a proper headmaster, brimming with certitudes. For my interview he sat behind a huge desk in an enormous leather chair and put me across from him in an equally enormous leather chair. I was the smallest of boys, late to grow, and the chair made me feel further diminished. I thought: this man knows a lot about authority, but he doesn't know much about boys. I still remember his name.

The next schools that we visited were little better; I felt the same chilly emanations from behind their armament of brick and ivy. If this was boarding school I wanted no part of it, and I was close to despair as we headed west across Massachusetts to our final stop. Deerfield Academy was the one school I hadn't heard much about. It was still a relative upstart in the higher tiers of secondary education, unencumbered by fame and sanctity.

My spirits lifted as soon as we turned off the highway into Old Deerfield. The historic houses along the village street were far gone in dilapidation—this was no shrine to the gods of upkeep—and the school had only two buildings made of sacred red brick. (A third one, the gym, would later reveal itself.) Otherwise it was a grab bag of serviceable wooden buildings of odd shapes and sizes. Some had obviously been pieced together from other buildings or moved from some-where else. I thought it would be a fine place to spend the next four years.

If the school didn't look like a proper school, the head-master didn't look like a proper headmaster. Nobody would have picked out Frank Boyden as a headmaster or noticed him in a crowd. He was an unusually small man, with a plain face, slicked-down black hair and metal-rimmed glasses. He met us at his house and we strolled over to his office. His walk was a kind of amble; nothing about it suggested that he was a monarch surveying his domain. He just inhabited the space where he happened to be—a natural feature of the New England landscape, like the elms that towered over us and the hills that framed the Deerfield River valley. He was first of all a Yankee, not first of all a headmaster.

His office was also not an office. It consisted of a desk just off the main corridor of the main classroom building; students going to and from their classes had to walk through his office several times a day. For my interview he pulled up two plain chairs and we sat down to talk. He soon learned that baseball was my first interest—almost my only interest—and that's what we talked about. He spoke with a slight Yankee twang and a dry Yankee wit. That was the best news of all; I never want to turn myself over to anyone who doesn't have a sense of humor. Steering the subject away from baseball, he told me a little about his school. Then he said that if I would like to come to Deerfield in the fall, there would be a place for me. I said I would very much like to come.

⊄ One thing to notice as you read this piece is that it's small. It's a pencil sketch, not an oil painting. Entire books have been written about Frank Boyden—most famously, John McPhee's *The Headmaster*—and some have been written about the school itself. In a memoir the only thing I could do was to recall what the school was like to *me*. Other alumni, given the same assignment, would have recalled what it was like to *them*, and their stories—probably quite different from mine—would have been equally valid. Be content to tell your small portion of a larger story. Too short is always better than too long. ℭ

I grew up with three older sisters in an isolated neighborhood that tweaked Mendel's law by having no other boys. I needed male friends—enough, at least, to form two baseball teams—but I was wary of the strict regimentation that I had hated at summer camp and assumed was every headmaster's controlling method. As it turned out, when I got to Deerfield I found that the school didn't have any written rules and the headmaster didn't seem to have any controlling method. There were no admonitory lectures, no threats of punishment.

Actually we were held under tight control. Attendance was taken at every class and every study hall, at all three required meals, at the required afternoon sport, at the required evening meeting, and at bedtime. The meeting was held after dinner in the large downstairs room of the Old Dorm—a room just big enough to hold the entire student body. We sat uncomfortably on the floor, pressed against each other, knees raised, and listened to the day's announcements and athletic results. On Sunday evening we sang hymns. The size of that room, I often thought, was the main determinant in the headmaster's admissions policy. If his school ever grew too large to come together every 24 hours as an intimate community, it would lose what made it unique. The meeting would end with Mr. Boyden mentioning the few things that were on his mind that day. His tone was conversational, almost offhand. But those casual remarks were in fact the school's rules. We always knew exactly what "the head" would want us to do and wouldn't want us to do. The rules seldom got broken because the ruler was too subtle. Any rebel trying to strike back at the power structure would have a hard time figuring out where to land his punches.

Sports were required of every boy every weekday afternoon, and there was a team to fit every size. For two of my four years I played on every midget team: midget soccer, midget basketball and midget baseball. Yet our equipment was as good as the varsity's, and so were the buses that took us to all those schools—Williston, Suffield, Mount Hermon—whose playing fields I can still picture. The integrity of the effort was validated, whatever our level or talent.

Just as midget teams gave dignity to the undersized, "the bank" gave sanctuary to smokers. Probably it's safe to guess that Mr. Boyden didn't approve of boys smoking. But in the geography of his life he had seldom been out of sight of a tobacco barn; he knew that the leaf is an insistent nag. If a Deerfield boy absolutely had to smoke, a place would be found for him. The place that Mr. Boyden designated was hilariously inconvenient: a crude wooden bench at the top of the bank that sloped down to the Deerfield River, beyond the last playing field on the upper level, a walk of several hundred yards from the dining hall. Yet after every meal a small band of smokers could be seen heading out across the steppes, whatever the weather, their shoulders hunched against the winter winds. Even from a distance they looked like losers and outcasts. But those words were not in Mr. Boyden's frame of reference. He knew that every adolescent boy is a loser and an outcast in some area: socially or emotionally, scholastically or athletically. His school enabled us to be comfortable with our limitations and confident in our strengths. Within that community of male friends I never doubted my freedom to be myself.

❡ Specific detail is the foundation of nonfiction writing, and nowhere is it more important than in a memoir. You must enable us to picture the place where you grew up and the people who crossed your life. But mere recollection isn't good enough ("our house was on Spruce Street"). The facts must make a point. When I started writing this Deerfield memoir I had forgotten all about "the bank." The act of writing brought it back, and I immediately knew I wanted to use it, partly because I didn't think any other writer would single out a feature of the school so squalid and marginal. But to me it was a perfect symbol of Frank Boyden's genius as a headmaster. Over the decades he admitted to Deerfield hundreds of boys who had been written off by other schools—and often by their parents. He created a safe environment where they could find themselves at their own developmental pace, as most of them eventually did. The despised bank enabled me to tell that whole story in one paragraph. ❡

No diocese can function smoothly without an unquestioning priesthood, and no bishop ever had a more loyal core of priests than the men Mr. Boyden hired to execute his vision. Many of them, I suspect, were only adequate teachers, but they were good enough to hammer into us the essentials of the subject they taught. More important, they were successful as men—patient and caring, endlessly adaptable to whatever diocesan tasks they were assigned. Besides teaching a full schedule of classes, they served as resident dormitory masters, coached a sport, presided over a dining hall table and advised student activities like the newspaper and the debating team. Unmarried or late to marry, outrageously underpaid and overworked, they accepted their vows of poverty and celibacy and useful toil with a cheerful heart, apparently wanting nothing more than to please the boss.

Many of them would go on to become headmasters of other schools, including two of my favorite teachers and coaches, Walter Sheehan and Jim Wickenden, and one of them, Donald "Red" Sullivan, was Deerfield's other headmaster, de facto, quietly keeping watch over its standards and keeping the machinery oiled. As a Roman Catholic from working-class Holyoke, he was an outsider in our narrow world of Protestant preppies. But no other teacher so exemplified the plain strength of character that Mr. Boyden had in mind for all of us. As master of the John Williams House, where I lived in both my freshman and sophomore years, a callow and cautious boy, Red Sullivan guided us toward manhood without exploiting his own manhood. For our own good he never coddled us, and for his own ego he never bullied us. He was a man of natural grace.

The two courses that served me best in my life work as a

writer and editor were Charles Huntington Smith's advanced Latin and Bartlett Boyden's required English composition. Mr. Smith was a man so venerable that he looked like a 19th-century schoolmaster; recalling him now, I think of photographs of Darwin as an old man. He had silky white hair, a bushy white moustache and a white goatee, and he wore the black suit and high collar that befitted his age and dignity. But his eyes were young, and so was his passion for the classical world.

He had turned his classroom into a small outpost of ancient Rome. Huge framed photographs of the Roman Forum and the Colosseum hung on the walls, and he had sent away for plaster statues of various Roman gods. Hermes on tiptoe, beckoning the other gods, was on his desk, and the Winged Victory stood nearby, still sending her message about beauty and line down through the ages. Mr. Smith knew that the icons that inhabit the classrooms of our youth can exert a lifelong spell, and in my case he was right. When I got to Italy during World War II, I used my first five-day pass to hitchhike to Rome. It took me two days to get there and two to get back, over the Apennines in winter, but the day in between was one of the most memorable of my life. I knew my way around the Forum because I had stared all one year at that photograph. Although I always liked Latin, I didn't love it until I got to Mr. Smith's class, finally getting beyond Caesar's dreary wars and Cicero's prim orations to Virgil's *Aeneid* and Horace's odes, finally discovering that the wonderful language also had a wonderful literature. It was from Mr. Smith that I first glimpsed what was meant by "humanist" and "liberal education," and in a lifetime of travels no city has called me back as often as Rome.

My other useful course was third-year English, taught by Bartlett Boyden. Unrelated to the headmaster except as a believer in Yankee thoroughness, he was a bald, ruddy man with a jolly smile. What he was smiling about I never knew, for he was dead serious about expository writing. If Mr. Smith's Latin was a joyful voyage to the grandeurs of language, Bartlett Boyden's English was a joyless drill in the carpentry of putting one word after another. But it taught me the one lesson I would need to know: that the craft I wanted to learn would not be mastered without hard and steady application.

Somewhere between those two extremes was one other course that I would take with me into the world: senior French, taught by the urbane and genuinely humorous Charles "Babe" Baldwin. His course immersed us in the French literature that he loved. But every class began with a vocabulary test: 20 words plucked from the reading we had done as homework the night before. Only after our test papers had been collected could we proceed to the Gallic charms of Guy de Maupassant and Prosper Mérimée. Incrementally, however, that daily exam gave me a hoard of words that still come back to me when I need them in French-speaking countries, and I remember Babe Baldwin with gratitude. His was a quintessential Deerfield course, rigorously but enjoyably preparing us to go forth as educated men.

Some of my happiest moments were spent playing second base on Lloyd Perrin's junior baseball team—the closest I came to athletic respectability after so much midgethood. Mr. Perrin, a small man himself, coached the junior football, basketball and baseball squads, which consisted of boys who were good athletes but were too small for the varsity. I only knew Mr. Perrin as a coach, not as a classroom teacher, but he could just as easily have been Babe Baldwin teaching French. Both men worked from the same values, instilling the fundamentals but never forgetting that the game is supposed to be fun. Like Deerfield's other priests, he was a man without vanity, secure in his self-esteem, and I still think of him as the model coach. I met him 50 years later in the person of Jim Leyland, who was manager of the Pittsburgh Pirates when I wrote my baseball book *Spring Training*. As I sat in the Florida sunshine interviewing Leyland about his own values as a teacher, some part of me was back at Deerfield taking infield practice, waiting for Mr. Perrin to rap me a grounder. It wouldn't be too easy and it wouldn't be too hard—just far enough from where I was standing to make me stretch my capabilities.

¶ Notice that my piece is not finally about a school; it's about people. In much of your memoir writing you will want to recall an institution that was important to you: a school, a church, a business, a volunteer organization. But institutions and places have no life of their own. You must bring them to life with men and women and children. Only a few places get written about solely as places. The point of Niagara Falls is the falls, not the people who went over them in a barrel. The point of

East Africa is the animals. The point of the Grand Canyon—well, I'll leave that to some theologian. If you're writing for an outdoor magazine your readers will want you to describe the fishing stream, the woodland trail, the skiing slope, the view from the top of the mountain; the place is the point. Otherwise, the point is people. Look for the human connection as you make your journey. Connect us to the people who connected with you. ❧

My other happiest moments were spent, as managing editor of the *Deerfield Scroll*, going to the town of Greenfield every two weeks to "make up" the paper at E. A. Hall & Company, whose indulgent printers, Herb and Bert, let me set the handsome Bodoni Bold headlines. Once Bert even allowed me to set a few lines on the holy Linotype. I could hardly wait for those Wednesday afternoons to arrive. It now occurs to me that I was one of the very few Deerfield boys to break out of the cocoon of the old village and make contact with the American workplace. The intoxicating smell of a printing shop would lead me by the nose to my first job—on the *New York Herald Tribune*—after I came home from the war. In retrospect I see that Deerfield prepared me to be a generalist when I grew up. I've always loved being a generalist in a society that prefers narrow expertise; there's no better education for a writer. When I went on to college I pursued many specialized courses of my own choosing. At Deerfield we were held to one educator's balanced menu for a well-rounded life.

Every Deerfield boy of a certain vintage has his favorite snapshot of that educator: Frank Boyden driving his horse and buggy, Frank Boyden coaching the football team inside an enormous fur coat, Frank Boyden exhorting us to "be mobile" (pronounced "mo-beel") on weekends when parents were expected, by which he meant that we should be alert to their needs and ready to improvise a solution to any crisis. I like to remember Mr. Boyden as a movie fan. Every Saturday night, except when the basketball team had a home game, he provided a first-run movie for us, always preceded by two new Mickey Mouse cartoons. Our theater was the rickety old barn behind the headmaster's house. The only seats with good visibility were in the rear, and as soon as the Saturday night meeting adjourned we sprinted to the barn at track-meet speed, knocking into each other in the darkness and slipping on the cinders of Albany Road. All those Hollywood films were still another layer of mulch laid down at Deerfield that I would be grateful for as an adult; part of my career at the *Herald Tribune* was spent as its movie critic.

But my favorite snapshot of Mr. Boyden in that role is connected with weekdays in the dead of winter when it was raining instead of snowing. The ski slope was muddy, the hockey rink was slush, the athletic program shut down. On those afternoons a study period was held to keep us productively occupied. But sometimes it rained for several days, and Mr. Boyden took pity. Slipping into the study hall, he would materialize at the front of the room and tell us he had a few announcements.

Finally, with the timing of George Burns, he would say, "I

just spoke on the phone with Mr. Lawler in Greenfield . . ." Cheers and shouts drowned him out. Mr. Lawler! Did the owner of that second-string movie theater ever know what hosannas greeted his name? When silence was restored Mr. Boyden said that—if we promised to be "orderly"—Mr. Lawler had a film he could lend us, and soon all schoolboy cares were washed away in balm from Hollywood. For a few hours we could imagine that we were Ronald Colman courting Madeleine Carroll in *The Prisoner of Zenda*, or Clark Gable defying Captain Bligh in *Mutiny on the Bounty*. Mr. Lawler had brought us the priceless gift of celluloid. I can't picture the headmasters of any of those other schools—the ones I knew I didn't want to attend—being mobile enough to rent a movie on a rainy afternoon.

One last point: my memoir has unity of point of view. It's told from the perspective of the boy I was at Deerfield, not the grown-up I was when I wrote it. This question—what age should I write my memoir from?—is often troublesome to memoir writers. Let's say you want to write about your childhood as you remember it. But you still live in the town where you grew up—you go to parent meetings in your old elementary school, you still visit the lake where your family went on vacation. Today the lake is not so idyllic, with all those shorefront developments and jet-skis, and the school has lost its terrors—it's just a building. The world has changed, and so has your way of looking at it. How will this affect your memoir?

Many years ago, in a memoir of my own childhood, I explained that my grandmother was a stern presence in our lives. A second-generation German-American, she never lost the Germanic relish for telling people off, and she had many didactic maxims to reinforce her point. *"Kalt Kaffee macht schön,"* she would declare, wagging her forefinger, leaving us to deconstruct the dreadful message. "Cold coffee makes beautiful," it said, as if hot coffee were some kind of self-indulgence, or perhaps a known cause of ugliness. *"Morgen Stund hat Gold im Mund"* ("The morning hour has gold in its mouth"), she would say to grandchildren who slept late. Frida Zinsser was a woman of fierce pride, bent on cultural improvement for her family, and in my memoir I duly noted her strength. But I also made it clear that she was no fun.

After the memoir was published, in a book called *Five Boyhoods*, my mother tried to set me straight. "Grandma wasn't really like that," she said, defending the mother-in-law who had made her own life far from easy. "She was unhappy and really quite shy, and she wanted to be liked." Maybe so; when I was older I could understand the bitter disappointments that made her the way she was. But she was like that to *me*—and that's the only truth a memoir writer can work with. Get your unities straight before you start. Choose one time frame—one version of your remembered truth—and stay with it. In my Deerfield memoir I break this rule several times to jump briefly ahead. I mention how the memory of Mr. Smith's Latin class sent me hurrying to Rome when I got to Italy as a G.I. and gave me a lasting love of the classical world. I also mention how Bartlett Boyden's arduous drills in clear writing gave me the tools I needed when I came home from the war and went to work for the *Herald Tribune*. Those two gifts had to be acknowledged: the act of teaching validated. One of the pleasures of writing a memoir is to repay the debts of childhood. Beyond that, it's important information for the reader. It's not enough to merely recall a teacher or a coach or an uncle or a neighbor who made a difference in your life. That's no small accomplishment. Take a few more sentences to tell us what the difference was.

But don't stay out in the future too long. The best memoirs are frozen in a particular time and place and social or historical condition. Russell Baker's *Growing Up* is about a boy and his mother contending with the Depression in New Jersey. Jill Ker Conway's *The Road from Coorain* is about a girl and her parents overwhelmed by a seven-year drought on a farm in the outback of Australia. Frank McCourt's *Angela's Ashes* is about a boy struggling with poverty in the slums of Limerick. Vladimir Nabokov's *Speak, Memory* is about a boy growing up in the twilight of czarist St. Petersburg—a kind of childhood that was about to end forever.

Alongside such cataclysmic events my four years at Deerfield were insular, untouched by reality. But they were what they were, and I tried to be true to them as I remembered them. That's all anyone writing about his or her life can hope to do.

3.

The Larger World

"**Y**OU'VE HAD SUCH AN interesting life. When are you going to write your memoir?" People have asked me that for years, and they're right about the interesting life. I've done many interesting kinds of work, visited many interesting places and met many interesting people.

The problem is that an interesting life doesn't make an interesting memoir. Only small pieces of a life make an interesting memoir. The rest is just getting through the day: going to work, raising a family, maintaining friendships, helping out in the community. Even people famous for having "an interesting life" didn't have an interesting life. Eisenhower and Churchill spent decades of servitude in the American peacetime army and the backwaters of British politics.

Instead of writing a memoir, I've cannibalized my life for its memorable moments, dropping them into my articles and books to give them a shot of freshness or surprise. Often I've used them when I was stuck for a lead that would be different from everyone else's lead. "Is there a story I can tell here?" I would ask myself. "Did anything ever happen to me that could jump-start this article in an unexpected way?" I'm always grateful to those ghosts from my past for turning up just when I need them. Always be on the lookout for narrative. Tell stories whenever you can. People love to be told stories.

Here's a story that I pressed into service in 1994 when I was sent to Normandy to write an article about the 50th anniversary of D-Day, the Allied landings on Omaha Beach. I knew that the anniversary would be massively covered by the media, and I assumed that their stories would focus on the landings themselves and on the crossing of the English Channel. My lead started on a whole other continent:

> The weeks before and after D-Day are still vivid to me because they come wrapped in a memorable image. I was a private in the American army, stationed near Algiers. French North Africa was a waiting room for the liberation of Europe, and when I visited Algiers I was struck by how many different Allied uniforms were walking around the city: Americans, Englishmen, Canadians, Australians, New Zealanders, Free French, Free Poles, Gurkhas, Brazilians, Senegalese and "Goums," fierce tribal warriors from France's military outposts in the Sahara. Wherever we came from, we were there for the same purpose. We were all waiting for

D-Day. The English and the Poles had been waiting since 1939.

One day when I went to Algiers I saw that a huge map had been erected across the facade of the main post office, several stories high. France was entirely green. Overnight, the map became the symbol of our collective hopes; people would gather in the square and just stare at it. Soon, we knew, the mighty armies and armadas massed in England would cross the channel. On June 6 the invasion finally took place, and when I next looked at the map I saw that some painters were working on it. They were putting white paint on the areas of the Normandy coast that the Allied armies had secured. Someday, the map said, all of France will be white.

I still remember what a familiar shape that peninsula became as we stared at the map, week after week, willing it to get whiter. I also remember how long it stayed green. The Allied armies were stalled by German divisions dug into the hedgerows of Normandy, and good news came only in fitful spurts: a white bulge spreading south to Saint-Lô, a white ribbon reaching east to Caen, a white arrow poking north to Cherbourg. Not until late July did the American and British divisions break out, and then the map exploded. Clusters of white arrows burst toward Paris, and by August 21 the map was white from the channel to the Seine. The crucial battle for Normandy was over; the final push to Germany could begin.

North Africa now emptied out. Some Allied units

landed in southern France and joined the sprint to the Rhine. My own unit went on to Italy. But D-Day remained the turning point of our war; for the first time it made the defeat of Hitler a foreseeable event. Thinking about it today and about the emotions it generated, I still see the map.

One reason I enjoyed using that story is that I've never seen it written or heard it told by anyone else. In the vast literature of World War II, am I the only person who was moved by that map and thought it worth writing about? I hope so. I like the idea that the story is mine alone, and I wish you the same pleasures of sole possession. Look for small anecdotes in the larger canvas of your life. They will help you to reduce to human scale the big events you've been caught up in. The invasion of Normandy was a mammoth event, involving vast numbers of people. My story reduces it to one 21-year-old soldier in Algiers. Any reader can identify with that American boy and with that moment in military history.

I was the sheltered son of northeastern WASPs living out America's last age of innocence and isolation. When my parents took my sister and me on a Grand Tour of Europe in the summer of 1939, it wouldn't have occurred to them to venture outside our cultural orbit. Our heritage was England and Europe, Greece and Rome; everything else was terra incognita. The churches we saw were Christian churches, the paintings we looked at were old masters, the languages we heard and tried to speak were the ones we studied in school. Sailing home on the *Statendam* in September, we heard over the radio that the Nazis had invaded Poland. But the news didn't have much reality; it was someone else's war. Cocooned in our steamer blankets, we tried not to believe—or chose not to believe—that our own snug world was also coming to an end.

When I next crossed the Atlantic, five years later, it was on a troopship called the *General Mann*. I was one of several thousand GIs stacked high on canvas bunks; no steward brought us bouillon in midmorning or tea in midafternoon. I had left Princeton, another WASP cocoon, to enlist in the army—a final snipping of the umbilical cord. I had no ambition to be an officer, and the army obliged me in that democratic whim. For almost a year I was shunted to training camps in the South so wet and dismal that I finally asked to be sent overseas, hoping to land in a place that was warm and dry—and interesting. The gamble paid off one day when I saw from the decks of the *General Mann* a white city rising out of the ocean. The city turned out to be Casablanca. Darkness had fallen by the time we went ashore, and we were taken by truck to an army base outside the city, where we bedded down in tents.

In the morning I awoke to a landscape that has been with me ever since. The land was a bold green, the sky was bluer than blue, and all the buildings were white, shimmering in the sun. Outside the camp fence, white-robed Arabs were riding donkeys along a road from a nearby village. I couldn't believe I was in North Africa. "It's just like the Bible!" we all exclaimed, using that simple-minded phrase, as travelers to Arab lands always have, to express something more complex: "This land looks older than any land I've seen before, and stirs deeper emotions."

The next day we were loaded onto a train consisting of "forty-and-eights," decrepit wooden boxcars first used by the French army in World War I to carry forty men or eight horses. The words QUARANTE HOMMES OU HUIT CHEVAUX were still stenciled on every car, and the straw we were supposed to sleep on was faintly scented of *chevaux*. Eight horses would have found it easier than forty men to find room to lie down at the same time. It was the most uncomfortable ride of my life—and the best. For six days I sat in the open door of that boxcar with my feet hanging out over Morocco, Algeria and Tunisia, not wanting the trip to end. Our ancient French engine was also in no hurry to arrive—it often stopped to rest going through the Atlas Mountains. I can still hear its high, self-important whistle.

Everything was new to me; nobody in my upbringing or my education had ever mentioned the Arabs. I loved the Arab sounds and smells in the air and the Arab names of the towns—Fez, Oujda, Sidi-bel-Abbès—and the Arab hubbub at the stations, and I romanticized the Arabs themselves. Who were these exotic people running alongside our train and clamoring around us when it stopped, and how had they expelled themselves from Mecca across such vast distances?

I finally came to roost with an air force unit near the Algerian town of Blida. The base was an hour's drive from Algiers, and I loved to visit that graceful white city, climbing up a hill around a crescent harbor. It was *my* city to discover and possess; nobody I knew had been there before me. Its architecture was French: tree-shaded boulevards, sidewalk cafes and kiosks, apartments with balconies on every floor. But I never thought I was in France. Arab men drove donkeys alongside French trolleys, black-veiled Arab women scuttled among French colonial wives, and the acrid smells of coffee and tobacco hung in the air. Most mysterious of all, at the city's dark center, strictly off-limits to Allied troops, was that sinister labyrinth, the casbah.

I spent eight months in North Africa, and my romance never cooled. Since then I've been repeatedly drawn back to Islamic places—not only the big cities like Damascus and Cairo but the lonely outposts like Oman and Timbuktu. I became a lifelong traveler to remote places, proprietor of my own Grand Tour, under some compulsion to visit other cultures that I also didn't know anything about: Egypt and India and China and Brazil and the Middle East and Southeast Asia and Indonesia and Africa. Those civilizations taught me to look and listen differently, to think in new ways about art and architecture, music and dance. I've seen art where there was no museum to certify it: calligraphy dancing across the wall of a mosque, elegant pottery in African villages, ornate silver jewelry on Asian tribal women. I've sat through an infinite variety of religious experiences and felt the spirit at work. I've heard Balinese gamelan music and African drumming that I wouldn't trade for Beethoven.

And it all began with a train ride across North Africa. As war stories go, it's a small one, but it was a big story to me. It changed how I thought about the world. Don't overlook the seemingly small stories in your life that shaped the person you turned out to be.

In the fall of 1944 my unit moved to Italy, and in that smashed and destitute country we hunkered down for the long winter. I was stationed far behind the battle lines, doing clerical work, my days spent in the exquisite tedium of army life. Being spared the agony and blood of combat was my ultimate lucky break, as I've been reminded ever since by the writers and poets of my generation who weren't so lucky: Paul Fussell, Samuel Hynes, Gardner Botsford, Harvey Shapiro and many others. Theirs is the true literature of World War II in its honesty and its compassion.

In May 1945 the war against Germany finally ended, and the army didn't have anything for its troops in Italy to do; the ships that might have brought us home were diverted to the war against Japan. Months of boredom stretched out ahead of us. One day I saw an item in the *Stars and Stripes* announcing that the army was establishing a college in Florence. Only one man per unit would be allowed to attend, and I ran to the adjutant to be the first to apply. My newspaper-reading habit paid off, and on the first of July I went off to college.

Our campus was an aeronautical academy just outside Florence that Mussolini had built, and for our faculty the army had recruited every officer and soldier in the Mediterranean theater who had been a teacher in civilian life. My dormitory window framed a perfect view across the red tile roofs of Florence to Brunelleschi's dome and Giotto's campanile. I knew nothing about art, so I signed up for art history courses. In the mornings I would hear lectures and see slides of the great works of the Renaissance, and in the afternoons, which we had off, I saw the great works themselves. The Florentines had begun to bring out of hiding the art treasures they had concealed from the Nazis, and sometimes I would see those works being hauled through the streets and put back in place; I looked Cellini's Perseus in the eye as it was hoisted onto its pedestal. It was a re-Renaissance: art belonged to the people again, as it had in the time of the Medicis. In September the college sent me back to my unit and I was given six certificates listing the courses I had taken and the grades I received. But only I knew how much they certified.

In November a troopship finally came to Naples and took me and 5,000 other men home, and I went to Princeton for an interview with the university official who would review my record. When I left college I had accumulated a grab bag of wartime credits that almost added up to a B.A. degree. Now I had three more, which Princeton granted just for serving in the armed forces, plus my army certificates. Originally I had thought I would want to return to Princeton for one more term to round out my fragmented college years. Now I only wanted to get on with whatever I was going to do next.

I was nervous as I walked across the campus to Nassau Hall, clothed in 200 years of historic ivy. The certificates I was clutching suddenly looked crude. Worst of all, I learned that my interview would be with Dean Root. Dean Root! I might as well get back on the train. Robert K. Root, dean of Princeton's faculty and guardian of its academic honor, was the prototype old professor. I had taken his lecture course in Augustan literature and had listened, week after week, as he excavated with dry precision the buried ironies of Jonathan Swift and the unsuspected jests of Alexander Pope, which even then we continued not to suspect. It never occurred to me that we would ever meet, and I was sorry to be meeting him now. He looked just as stern up close.

Dean Root studied my Princeton transcript and then looked at my army certificates. He said he had never seen anything like them; I was the first veteran to show up from one of the army's postwar colleges. Then he studied my transcript again and made some notes. Then he studied the army certificates again and made more notes. He was scowling and mumbling. I could see that he was adding up my credits and that they weren't adding up to a B.A. degree. He shook his head and mumbled that I seemed to be a little short. I told myself I was a dead duck.

Then, suddenly, I was no longer being examined by a dean. A real person was sitting across from me, his features not unkindly, and he asked me what I had done during the war. I found myself telling him about my year in North Africa and how it opened my eyes to the Arab world. I told him about my hitchhiking trips to Rome, and about seeing *La Bohème* in the Naples opera house, and about my Renaissance summer in Florence, and about the weekend jaunts I made to Pisa and Lucca and Siena to look at their art and architecture.

The dean's face clouded over. "Tell me," he said, "I suppose Siena was mostly destroyed during the war." I realized that I was the first returning soldier to bring him news of the beautiful old city. Suddenly I understood what Siena would mean to this quintessential humanist; probably he had first seen it as a young man himself. Suddenly it was possible to understand that Dean Root had once been a young man. I told him that Siena hadn't been touched by the war and that the great striped *duomo* was still there on its hilltop, as it had been since the 12th century, visible to travelers from miles away.

Dean Root smiled fleetingly and saw me to the door and said Princeton would inform me of its decision soon. Two weeks later he wrote to say that I had passed Princeton's requirements for a degree and that I could receive my diploma at a special winter graduation for returning servicemen. I've always thought he waived one or two credits to make my total come out right. In the middle of the interview he decided to stop counting; numbers weren't as important to him as learning. In January I went to Princeton and rented a cap and gown and received my dubious B.A. Not long afterward I got the job that had been my boyhood dream—working for the *New York Herald Tribune*—and began my career as a journalist. Dean Root had freed me to get on with my life.

That half hour in Nassau Hall has stayed with me ever since. I, too, have never believed in numbers. One of the corrosive forces in American life, I think, is our obsession with the victorious result: the winning Little League team, the high test score, the record-breaking salary, the sacred bottom line. Coaches who finish first are gods; coaches who finish second are not. Less glamorous gains made under good coaches and good teachers—growth, wisdom, confidence, self-expression, sportsmanship, dealing with failure and loss—aren't valued because they don't get a grade. One of my most-reprinted articles, a column for *Look* in 1967, pleaded for the right to fail—one of the few freedoms America doesn't grant its citizens, especially its young people:

We need mavericks and dreamers and dissenters far more than we need junior vice presidents, but we paralyze them by insisting that every step be a step up to the next rung of the ladder. Yet often the only way for boys and girls to find their proper road is to take a hundred side trips, poking out in different directions, faltering, pulling back and starting again.

"But what if we fail?" they ask, whispering the dreaded word across the generation gap to their parents, back in the Establishment. The parents whisper back, "Don't!"

What they should say is: "Don't be afraid to fail." Failure isn't the end of the world. Countless people have had a bout of failure and come out stronger as a result. Many have even come out famous. History is strewn with eminent dropouts, loners who followed their own trail, not worrying about its unexpected twists and turns because they had faith in their own sense of direction. To read their biographies is exhilarating, not only because they beat the system but because their system was better than the one they beat.

In the 1970s, when I was master of one of Yale's residential colleges, I was the shepherd to a flock of 400-odd bright young men and women who were so stressed by the fear of less-than-perfect grades that they had almost forgotten how to live. I made it my mission to nudge those students out of their numerical prison and get them to try their wings. Dean Root was always somewhere in the room when I did.

World War II was the turning point in my life, broadening what I knew and how I thought about the world. But the only stories I ever wrote about the war are the two I've briefly retold here: one about a train ride across North Africa, the other about a summer in Florence. Neither is about the war itself. They are stories about how the war changed *me*.

Remember this when you write about your own life. Your biggest stories will often have less to do with their subject than with their significance: not what you did in a certain situation, but how that situation affected you. *Walden* isn't really a book about how Henry David Thoreau spent his days at Walden Pond. It's about what went through his head for two years at Walden Pond.

4.

A Sense of Enjoyment

O F THE 13 YEARS I spent at the *New York Herald Tribune* after I came home from the war, ten were spent in the journalistic crannies of show business. That phase of my life began one day in 1948 when the managing editor, George Cornish, called me into his office to say that the venerable drama editor, a man who looked like Edmund Gwenn playing Santa Claus in *Miracle on 34th Street*, was being retired and that a thorough overhaul of the Sunday drama section was wanted. Would I be interested? I was then an editor on one of the other Sunday sections, as happy as only a 26-year-old journalism-struck kid could be. No larger dreams had yet come knocking.

But Mr. Cornish (I always called him Mr. Cornish) knew that his urbane newspaper could no longer get by with an entertainment section that looked like a relic from some

Jurassic age of typography, its pages a thicket of antique type-faces and borders and drawings and musty articles. He remembered that I was a fan of the Broadway musical theater and that I had written songs for the Princeton Triangle Club when I was in college. Whether I knew anything about the nonmusical theater he didn't ask. He offered me the job of drama editor, and I took it.

The *Herald Tribune* building, at 230 West 41st Street, was on a block that it shared with three parking lots, a garage, a theater that was usually dark, a bus terminal for buses that went to towns in New Jersey that not many people went to, a barbershop, and a store that sold tuxedos to waiters and musicians. The building extended through to 40th Street, where it had an employees' entrance that served more valu-ably as an exit, emerging only a few steps from the Artist & Writer's Restaurant, known as Bleeck's (pronounced Blake's), a former speakeasy with a mile-long bar that was a second home to the *Herald Tribune* staff. True to its lineage, it didn't allow the faithful to go dry on Election Day, when bars were legally closed. We were served our midday drink in a blue china cup in the back room.

Bleeck's had the lived-in look—oak paneling, a suit of armor, original Thurber drawings—of having been all things to all writers who ever worked for the *Herald Tribune*, many of whom, like John O'Hara and Joseph Mitchell and Nun-nally Johnson, were bound for greater glory. So fiercely was it regarded as a *Trib* preserve that reporters from the nearby *New York Times* seldom set foot in it, and there is no com-puting the number of man and woman hours spent there by

Trib people—before noon, at lunch, in midafternoon, at dinner, between editions and until 4 A.M.—in intense discussion of their trade and lubrication of their talents. I mention it not to romanticize still another Manhattan saloon—a genre that has no shortage of practitioners—but because it would be derelict to omit from any description of the paper an annex so vital to its life flow. When the presses rolled, the walls of Bleeck's trembled symbiotically, and reporters and editors would leave their martinis on the bar and go upstairs to check their stories in print. Their drinks would be waiting when they got back.

The *Herald Tribune's* city room was a vast and grimy place that got repainted every few years in a less restful shade of eye-rest green. The desks were crowded against each other and were charred with cigarette burns and mottled with the stains of coffee spilled from a thousand cardboard cups. In summer the air was sluggishly stirred by fans with dangling black wires that looked like the cables you see in the street after an electrical storm. In the center of the room the city editor, L. L. Engelking, a hulking perfectionist from Texas, bellowed his displeasure with the imperfect efforts of his staff. I thought it was the most beautiful place in the world.

My new domain, the drama department—my jurisdiction included the theater, movies, music, art, dance and radio—occupied one corner of the room. I had often wondered about its mysterious inhabitants: the florid older man staring into his typewriter for words that were no longer there (drama critic?), the lithe young man in a red turtleneck (music critic?), the pasty-faced man so seemingly unaccustomed to daylight (theater reporter?). I only knew the dance critic, Walter Terry, a fellow veteran who was also just out of the army. When he stood up to stretch he stood in fourth position.

Not long after I took up residence, the drama critic had one drink too many—he fell while walking down the aisle to his seat on opening night—and was replaced by Walter Kerr, who thereby became the third critical eminence in our midst, the others being the radio critic John Crosby and the music critic Virgil Thomson, who was then at the height of his power and influence. Over the years Thomson hired various young composers as part-time reviewers, including Paul Bowles, and on Wednesday afternoons they would drop in to get their assignments. I remember one day when Helen Reid, the *Herald Tribune*'s dowager owner, stopped to peer into the music department, where several critics were in a particularly *outré* state of dress and excitability. Mrs. Reid blinked in disbelief that such bizarre folk were on her payroll, but the apparition didn't go away, and she hurried on to saner territory. Soon afterward Paul Bowles moved to Tangier and never came back, perhaps driven by the squalor of the city room to seek the austerity of the desert, which his novels, like *The Sheltering Sky*, would so vividly capture.

The callers at my desk were mainly press agents for the Broadway plays and Hollywood movies that were about to open. They came to discuss possible articles for the Sunday section and to bring me photographs and movie stills that I might use in a layout. The Broadway theater was then an intimate community, and so was Hollywood—a company town dominated by a half-dozen major studios. Year after year I dealt with the same publicists for Broadway producers and for MGM, 20th Century Fox, Paramount, Columbia, Universal and United Artists, and I still think of them as friends. Although we were on opposite sides of the journalistic fence—they were the supplicants and I the dispenser—we were bound by mutual ties of respect, each with a job to do.

After six years as drama editor I switched desks and became the paper's movie critic for four years. I got up every morning and went to the movies. It was a decade of steady output: 300 Sunday drama sections and almost 600 movie reviews and Sunday columns. But I remember it as a time of high enjoyment. I had two seats on the aisle for every opening night on Broadway; I went on junkets to movie premieres in faraway places; I was taken on private tours of the Hollywood studios in the twilight of their golden years; I was invited to press receptions for movie stars I knew on the screen but didn't seem to know in person. "What did you think of Gary Cooper?" my wife asked after one such event. It turned out that he had been at our table. Cyd Charisse, whose lineaments I thought I had memorized, was seated next to me at a lunch in Sardi's. I found that out when the press agent introduced her as Cyd Charisse.

In 1959 I left the *Herald Tribune* to become a freelance writer, but I continued to write about show business with some frequency and to find it a world full of pleasant surprises. One of my first assignments was to interview the newly ascendant movie star Peter Sellers for *Life*. With the advent of wealth and fame Sellers had just bought a 16th-century manor house in a village called Chipperfield, north of

London, along with 50 acres of rolling Hertfordshire and the usual assortment of greenhouses and potting sheds. I found him in an ancient tithe barn, where previous lords of the manor had counted the livestock of their tenant farmers. He was laying 500 feet of track for a model railroad.

Another new comic genius I interviewed in the early 1960s, for the *Saturday Evening Post*, was Woody Allen. He had just begun to perform in nightclubs, and my article was the first long magazine piece written about him. Fifteen years later I had a second close encounter with Allen, which I described in an article called "My Stardust Memories." I still remember that when I started to write it I thought, "This is going to be fun." That's something I almost never think. I may think, This is going to be interesting, or unusual, or challenging, but I rarely think it's going to be fun. If you ever find that thought crossing your mind, run to your computer before it goes away. Given a choice between two projects—one that you feel you ought to write and one that sounds like fun—go for the one you'll enjoy working on. It will show in your writing. The reader should always think that the writer is feeling good.

Conveying a sense of enjoyment is one of my main goals as a writer, and I offer "My Stardust Memories" (below) as a specimen, along with some pedagogical thoughts on matters of tone and organization.

Every time a new Woody Allen movie comes along I can't help thinking back to one of his earlier films, *Stardust Memories*. That's the one that gave me my movie career.

The year was 1980, and I was sitting at my typewriter in New York, plying my writer's trade. When the phone rang I had no great expectations; freelance writers answering the phone tend to be braced for negative news.

"Bill, honey?" said a young woman's voice. "This is Sandra from Woody Allen's office. Woody wondered if you'd like to be in his new movie."

That was something new in phone calls. I had never done any acting or dreamed any theatrical dreams. But who didn't want to be in a Woody Allen movie? I knew that he often cast ordinary people in small roles. What small plum did he have for me? I hesitated for a decently modest moment and then told Sandra I'd like to do it.

"Good," she said. "Woody will be very pleased." She said that someone else would be calling me with further details.

A half hour later the phone rang again. "Bill, honey," a voice said, "this is Stephanie from Woody Allen's office." How wonderful, I thought, to be in a line of work where I was called "Bill, honey." Stephanie said she was calling to get my measurements. Measurements! I caught a whiff of greasepaint over the telephone line. She needed my jacket size, my waist size, my trouser length, my inseam and my collar size, and I gave them to her gladly. I would have told her anything. I wanted to ask what role I was being measured *for*, but she was gone. I called my wife to tell her I was in show business.

The next day the phone rang again. "Bill, honey," another voice said, "this is Jill from Woody's office." Jill explained that my scene was going to be shot on Friday morning at a film studio in uptown Manhattan. I should get there by 9 and check with the wardrobe people about my costume. Meanwhile I should also report to the movie's casting agent to have my picture taken and to fill out some forms.

The agent's office was on Central Park West, and the next day I went around to see her. She explained that she specialized in casting extras, and her walls were lined with photographs of extraneous-looking people. She was a woman who had seen a lot of faces, and as she stood me against a wall and peered into her Polaroid camera I thought I heard a small sigh.

"Where did Woody find *you?*" she asked.

❡ That lead does several jobs. First, it tells the reader: "I'm the tour guide and this is the trip I'm going to take you on." You know that you'll eventually hear the whole story and that all your questions—where *did* Woody find me?—will be answered. It also compels you to keep reading. That's what every writer wants his or her lead to do; it's better than the alternative. But above all it establishes the writer's personality, or persona. My lead creates a figure familiar in humor writing and travel writing: the writer as a patsy, a rube, someone a little out of his depth. This gives the reader the enormous pleasure of feeling superior.

It could be argued that I heightened my persona for comic effect—that I made myself more of a bumpkin than I am. That's true; I'm obviously having fun with the situation, keeping myself amused. Writing is such hard and lonely work that I look for any opportunity to cheer myself up. But on some level that invented person is really me. I *was* a little out of my depth. Sandra and Stephanie and Jill were sirens beckoning me to pleasures that were no part of my ordinary day. Hearing their voices on the phone, I was whisked back to my boyhood and to every conversation I had with girls who were infinitely taller and wiser. That invented self has a grain of truth. Moral: It's O.K. to crank your personality up to a higher notch of enjoyment. But don't exaggerate grossly; don't strain the reader's good will. Stay recognizable underneath.

Now my article must get down to real work: pure carpentry. The reader needs to know how Woody Allen and I first connected. ❡

In the winter of 1963 I got a call from an editor at *The Saturday Evening Post*. The magazine wanted an article about a new comic who was playing at a club in Greenwich Village; everyone said he was going to be the next big talent. Sure, sure, I thought. I asked what the comic's name was. It was Woody Allen. That didn't sound promising either. Still, I agreed to write the piece, and a few nights later my wife and I turned up at the Village Gate. It was a huge barn, depressingly dark and empty. But suddenly I became aware that an amazing jazz pianist was at work. Through the gloom I made out a pallid man in dark glasses, curled over the keyboard, caressing harmonies out of it that were cerebral but also highly emotional. "The comic's not going to be any good," I said, "but at least I've found a great piano player." It was Bill Evans, who would become the most influential jazz pianist of his generation.

The comic, however, was no less an original artist. A seemingly terrified young man, blinking out at the audience through black-framed glasses, Woody Allen at 27 was already a veteran of writing sketches for Sid Caesar and other giants of television's golden age of comedy. But as a performer of his own material he was still a novice; at his first gigs his manager had had to push him trembling onto the stage.

Allen's monologue consisted of telling the story of his life. It was the life of a chronic loser, told in a rapid salvo of jokes: "As a boy I was ashamed to wear glasses; I memorized the eye chart, and then on the test they asked essay questions." "I won two weeks at an interfaith camp, where I was sadistically beaten by boys of all races." The jokes, though simple, were unfailingly funny, and beneath the humor they were doing solid work as autobiography. This was a champion nebbish, one that every neurotic in America could—and soon would—identify with. Allen had invented a surefire formula for an anxious new age: therapy made hilarious. A few days later I interviewed him to learn the details of the life I had heard refracted in the jokes.

In 1970 I moved to New Haven to teach writing at Yale. During those years Allen not only came of age as a movie writer and director, with *Sleeper*, *Love and Death*, *Annie Hall*, *Interiors* and *Manhattan*. He emerged as a dazzling essayist, contributing almost 50 pieces to the *New Yorker* that raised literary humor to new altitudes. He was obviously a true descendant of his idol, S. J. Perelman, and I used his work in my teaching.

I knew that Allen had been a pioneer wearer of sneakers in fashion-proud Manhattan. At Yale I was seldom out of sneakers myself. But I was prepared to kick the habit when I returned to New York in the summer of 1979; I wasn't going to disgrace my native city. What I hadn't known was that during my decade away from New York its sartorial codes would disintegrate; people seemed to be walking around town in their underwear. I continued to wear a jacket and tie, but sneakers were on my feet more often than my upbringing would have thought proper.

One Saturday in the spring of 1980 I was walking down Madison Avenue. Suddenly my eyes seemed to fix on a pair of sneakers walking toward me, and the wearer of those sneakers seemed to fix on mine. It was as if the sneakers recognized each other. We both stopped, and I saw that it was Woody Allen. We stood on the sidewalk for a few minutes and talked about writing. Then we went our separate ways and I didn't give it any further thought. In Allen's brain, however, one last neuron must have fired, for it was only a few days later that Sandra called to ask whether I would like to be in Woody's new movie.

❡ So much for carpentry. The necessary details are out of the way, and the central narrative—the making of the movie—can begin. Always make sure your readers know what they need to know at every stage of the journey. That may require a change of location or chronology—in the case of the previous six paragraphs, a flashback. But that's why God gave writers the asterisk. Divide your piece into logical sections and separate them by an asterisk or a line space. That enables you to give proper energy to writing each section without succumbing to terror at the magnitude of the total task. Then put that section behind you and start fresh on the next one. Soon there will be no more sections left to write. My next three sections—pure storytelling—fell into place quite easily and enjoyably. ⌥

Promptly at 9 on Friday morning I showed up at the movie studio and was sent upstairs to a wardrobe room and given my costume. It was the habit of a Catholic priest. I thought of all my Protestant forebears; they would just have to understand that I was doing this for my art. The black robe and clerical collar fit me well, and I went downstairs feeling holy enough to administer a sacrament. Woody Allen was standing on the set, which was the interior of a shabby passenger train.

"Do I look spiritual enough for you?" I asked.

"Those aren't spiritual glasses," he said. The director of the visually impeccable *Interiors* wasn't going to have a Catholic priest wearing the horn-rimmed spectacles of an Ivy League WASP. He called for a prop woman, who came with a cardboard box full of glasses. Picking fastidiously among them, Allen fished out exactly the pair that would be worn by the priest of a blue-collar parish in Queens. They were made of chrome, with wide side-pieces, and they were ugly. I looked at myself in a mirror. There was no sign of the kindly face that normally gazed back at me. The man in the mirror was an unforgiving agent of God.

What was being filmed was the opening sequence of the movie *Stardust Memories*, which served as a prologue to the movie itself. It took the form of a surrealist fantasy. Two trains are proceeding on parallel tracks. One is full of beautiful people and one is full of ugly people. Woody Allen is trapped on the ugly people's train, and he looks with longing at the people on the other train: handsome men in white flannels and boaters with tennis racquets and croquet mallets, laughing women in long white dresses and Gibson-girl hats, twirling parasols.

Frantic to get off the losers' train, Allen begins by pulling on the bell cord. His efforts lead only to entanglement. Next he appeals to the conductor, showing him his ticket and pointing to the adjacent train. The conductor studies the ticket impassively and hands it back. Desperate, Allen scans the rows of ugly passengers and sees one last hope of salvation: a Catholic priest. That was my big moment.

The sequence took all morning to film. There was the usual quest for perfection: the fussing with lights and sound, the reshooting of scenes that didn't satisfy Allen or his cinematographer, Gordon Willis. Finally it was time for my scene, and Allen gave me my instructions: I was to show no emotion when he approached me as a supplicant. It was the best possible directing advice for someone who has no idea how to act and would ruin a scene by trying to; when a photographer asks me to smile I contort my cheeks in a weird simulacrum of mirth. But to show *no* emotion is easy; anyone can keep his face blank. It's also the ultimate nightmare for any petitioner seeking help.

Without boasting, I can say that I gave Allen no glimmer of hope. No matter how many takes were required to solve Gordon Willis's technical problems, some of which were related to a jouncing mechanism that made the train appear to be moving, my performance was steely in its discipline, and when it was over—all six seconds of it—I gladly turned in my ecclesiastical garb. I had the rest of my life to look back on my movie career.

But it wasn't over. Several months later the phone rang and a familiar voice said, "Bill, honey, this is Sandra at Woody Allen's office. We need you for another scene."

Sandra explained that the final destination of the ugly people's train is a city dump, where everyone wanders across acres of garbage. The scene had been filmed the previous fall at a dump in New Jersey, but the weather was so cold that everyone's breath was showing. Allen wanted to shoot it again, this time at the main New York City dump next to Jamaica Bay, near Kennedy airport, the biggest dump in the world. As a late addition to the cast of train passengers I was needed among the dump-walkers. Sandra said the bus would leave from Vesey Street, in lower Manhattan, at 5:30 A.M. the following Tuesday. Could I be there?

"I'll be there," I said. "What about my costume?"

"Not to worry," she said.

On Tuesday morning, earlier than I've reported for any task since World War II, I found a large bus parked in the pre-dawn darkness of Vesey Street. Most of the ugly people were already on the bus; extras are so dependent on their occasional day's work, one of them told me, that they take no chance of being late. Their aspiration is to graduate to a "five-liner," the next higher union job, which calls for five lines of dialogue. During our long day together, also reminiscent of the army in its endless waiting, I found them to be men and women of infinite resignation and good cheer.

Our bus took us across the East River and through the lightening streets to a senior citizens' center near Far Rockaway, where, in a recreation room, our costumes were hanging on coat racks. Seeing my priest's robe and chrome glasses waiting for me, I understood that in film production, as in baseball, it's not over till it's over; costumes stay rented for the duration. I changed into my holy attire and several of the extras called me "Father" and asked for a blessing. The sun finally came up.

Back on the bus, we proceeded to the dump, a vast range of hills made entirely of garbage. Sanitation trucks kept arriving with garbage from all over the city and seagulls came screaming down to meet them. It was an ideal landscape for a surrealistic movie: a place at the end of the world, alien and desolate. We were told that Woody Allen had visited the dump the previous day to decide where he wanted to shoot our walk. He chose a spot where the garbage was piled in a configuration that pleased his artistic eye, and that's where our bus now arrived to meet him.

But all was not well. Allen had forgotten that garbage doesn't hold still. Monday's picturesque formations had been compacted under new truckloads of trash, and the view that greeted him on Tuesday wouldn't do. Shooting would be delayed until he got the garbage rearranged. City Hall had evidently told the Sanitation Department to cooperate with the filmmakers, for soon we saw trucks with new garbage making their way up the mountain toward us. Galvanized by their approach, Allen turned into Toscanini, conducting each driver to where he wanted the load dumped, until at last a towering wall of garbage had risen not far from where we were standing. The air was scented with the refuse and unfinished meals of seven million New Yorkers, and new gulls descended in noisy armadas. Woody was satisfied.

Our assignment as outcasts from the ugly people's train was to trudge aimlessly across the garbage, looking dazed and forlorn. That wasn't hard to do; we were in a land of lunar strangeness. Underfoot, the terrain was damp and fetid, grabbing at our shoes. Allen placed his camera so that we would be framed against the new wall of garbage. It loomed behind us like a mountaineer's cliff, sealing us off.

So began what would stretch into hours of walking on the dump. On one level it was one of the most interesting days I've ever spent, well outside the normal experience of a lifetime. Cinematically, however, it was tedious work. The skies were gray, and the sporadic sun reflected off the garbage unevenly. Allen and Willis wanted to make sure that the sequences they shot would match each other in quality of light and density of seagull. They shot us from a distance, straggling across the tundra, and they shot us in close-up when we came near, our faces etched with loathing at our fate. But perfection eluded them, and at midday we were sent off for a lunch break.

When we came back the unthinkable had happened: our

gulls were gone. Fleets of sanitation trucks were dumping new loads about 100 yards away, and our seagulls had flown over to get a fresher meal. We needed new gulls so that the afternoon scenes would match the morning scenes. Word went out, trucks arrived with new garbage to top off our old garbage, and the gulls came screaming back. Shooting resumed, and in midafternoon, on a peak in Queens, my movie career really did come to an end.

❡ Those two sections cover a lot of territory: two complicated days of making a movie with a major director and cinematographer. But—to re-emphasize my point about asterisks—I wasn't overwhelmed by the prospect of getting the stories told because I thought of them as two separate stories, not one continuous narrative. I moved sequentially through the first story—filming the scene on the train—and put it aside. Then I turned my attention to the next story—filming the scene at the dump—and moved sequentially through *that* narrative. That left only the short final section (below), which wraps things up—another separate story. Always look for ways to break your long projects into manageable chunks of writing time and energy. ❡

Stardust Memories opened in September, and a few days before the premiere my phone rang. "Bill, honey," a voice said, "this is Beverly at Woody Allen's office. There's going to be a private screening tomorrow night at the Coronet Theater for everyone who was connected with the picture. You're welcome to come and bring any guests." I called my wife and children, and the next night we all went to the Coronet to see Daddy in the movies.

Around me I recognized many of my fellow uglies from the train and the dump. But we weren't the only freaks in the theater. Uglies were everywhere! It was as if we had been sprinkled with some mutational dust as we walked through the lobby. To my relief, the lights went down and the movie began. I was nervous—would my debut be a success?—but soon the worst was over. In the scene on the train my face was stern enough to scare even a venial sinner, and when it later reappeared in a huge close-up at the dump I was proud to see that it was still unleavened by the quality of mercy. I could relax and enjoy the rest of the film.

Actually it was a querulous movie, not all that enjoyable. Allen plays a comedy writer who yearns to be taken seriously as an artist. Instead he is hounded by his adoring fans at a film festival in the Catskills and at other public appearances, the resentful prisoner of his fame. Like its prologue, the movie took an owlish view of humanity. All those fans swarming over Allen—the Hieronymous Bosch school of filmmaking—were as ugly as the passengers on the train and at the dump. Now I understood who all those men and women in the theater were; the casting agent had done her job well. When the movie ended and the audience spilled out onto the sidewalk, pedestrians strolling up Third Avenue paused in wonderment at so much genetic disarray.

After the film was released I heard from some of my former Yale students. As master of one of Yale's largest colleges for six years, I knew a large number of undergraduates. When I handed them their diplomas they had every right to expect that I wouldn't keep popping into their lives as an authority figure. But it was their bad luck to be Woody Allen's natural constituency, and as soon as *Stardust Memories* opened they flocked to see it. Every time my grim clerical visage jumped out of the giant screen, I was told, startled cries went up from various parts of the theater. It was the sound of Mother Yale's sons and daughters regressing to the womb.

I was sorry to have caused them such a traumatizing moment. But as I look back on my movie career I have one larger regret. I never got called "Bill, honey" again.

5.

Writing About Places

I N MAY 1954 I finally saw the girl I wanted to marry. Across a crowded cocktail party Caroline Fraser gave me the best smile I ever received. She was tall and blonde and beautiful— and also, it turned out, bright and funny. I asked her if I could take her to dinner, and we walked out into the streets of Manhattan and began our life together. She was from the Midwest and was working for *Life* as a reporter. A month later I made a double proposal: that we get married and take a trip across the heart of Africa. I pointed out that Niagara Falls was old hat for honeymooners; Stanley Falls would be something different. I coaxed an extra month of vacation out of the *Herald Tribune*'s managing editor, George Cornish, in return for which I would write some articles from a part of the world that his paper was too poor to cover. I particularly promised to write a series of pieces on the brutal Mau Mau uprising in Kenya, which was then in its third year. That would also be something new in honeymoons. Caroline didn't blink—then or ever again—and in October, duly married, we set out, sailing on a ship of dubious registry to Lisbon, where we took a slow plane to the Congo.

We caught Africa at the very end of an era, just before two revolutions that would forever change its equilibrium. One was the tide of nationalism that washed the colonial powers out. The other was the advent of jet planes, which would bring hordes of tourists to a continent where only individual travelers had gone before. But Caroline and I knew nothing of such coming events. Our Africa was still a creature of 19th-century Europe, stamped with its ambitions and its possessive names. The Congo where we began our journey was the *Belgian* Congo, its capital city of Leopoldville named for a Belgian king. In my imagination, as we droned over the matted jungle in a Belgian DC-3, the entire continent was a Victorian invention; the British novelist H. Rider Haggard had first put the spell of Africa on me as a boy with *King Solomon's Mines*. When we put down for the night at Stanleyville I felt that we were at the absolute center of "darkest Africa." Even the *Princeton Alumni Weekly* wouldn't find me here.

As we walked toward the shack that served as a terminal, I saw a short, plump man in safari clothes standing in the doorway. His features were concealed by a pith helmet that came down to his horn-rimmed glasses, which in turn met a thick moustache and a beard. When we got nearer he waved casually and said "Hi, Bill." It was Art Buchwald, the *Herald Tribune* humor columnist. He was there to write an article for

Collier's in the macho Ernest Hemingway style: "Every man must get his water buffalo—otherwise he can't live with himself." We bought Buchwald a beer at our hotel, which was called the Pourquoi Pas, and in the morning he set off for the interior. I never did find out whether he got his buffalo.

The next day our plane continued on and brought us to Usumbura, a small city in the Belgian protectorate of Ruanda-Urundi, the scenic land of the Watusi, which we hoped to tour. (Later it would be divided into the new countries of Rwanda and Burundi.) Our idea was to hire a car with a European driver, and we began by studying a map in the lobby of the Paguidas Hotel. Most of the roads were annotated with local hazards: "Lions rather troublesome," "Shaky cable ferry over 200-foot gorge," "Buffalo, leopards, sleeping sickness, bridges doubtful." It turned out that the only car for hire was a 1935 Plymouth, its driver a young African who spoke a few words of what we optimistically took to be French. That evening at the bar, while scratchy Ruth Etting records blared "Mean to Me" and "Melancholy Baby" into the African night, a Belgian colonial told us we would be "bloody fools to drive around this country with a native boy." But we chose to be bloody fools and were rewarded with a four-day circuit of Lake Kivu that was a mixture of pastoral beauty, handsome people, pidgin French and automotive repair. The seven-foot-tall Watusi, as certified by MGM in *King Solomon's Mines*, were nature's aristocrats.

Next we flew to Uganda and entered the British orbit. Uganda was a protectorate of Great Britain and a keeper of its memories; its two great lakes were Victoria and Albert.

From there we took a plane to Kenya. The airline stewardess gave us a copy of the *East African Standard*, noting that it had "many lovely features." If it did, I never saw them. My eye was caught by the headline: WHITE MAN BURIED ALIVE IN MAU MAU VOODOO SACRIFICE. A Mau Mau gang had broken into the home of Dr. A. G. A. Leakey, an old Kenya settler and friend of the Kikuyu tribe, killed his wife and taken him off, later to be buried alive—a necessary ritual, according to a Mau Mau priestess, if their revolt was to succeed. What it meant was that the terrorist movement had fallen into the hands of witch doctors.

Nairobi in 1954 was like a movie town of the Old West, its paved streets relapsing into dirt at the edge of town. British Tommies patrolled the streets with Sten guns, and the New Stanley Hotel looked like an arsenal. British farmers in from the "white highlands" laid their pistols on the bar, and wives arriving for dinner wore guns on their evening gowns. But it was still every inch a British colony, the land of white master and black servant depicted by Isak Dinesen. Jomo Kenyatta, the alleged guru of the Mau Mau movement, with its blood oath binding the Kikuyus to purge the land of whites, was safely locked away in jail. Ten years later he would be the first president of the new nation of Kenya.

We began our stay by doing the usual tourist things: visiting the large game reserve outside town and drinking tea. "Guests," one brochure admonished us, "are expected to conform to the tea-drinking habits of the colonial British, which begin at 6:30 A.M., when a cup of tea is delivered to the bedside by the room boy." There was no question of not conforming;

tea arrived at dawn despite all preventive efforts. Shifting into journalistic gear, I presented myself to the British authorities. They told Caroline and me that their troops had finally driven the Mau Mau out of Nairobi to hideouts in the Aberdare forest and on the slopes of Mount Kenya; if we wanted to see the front we should go to Nyeri. Nyeri was the site of Treetops Hotel, where tourists once flocked to watch wild game at night and where Princess Elizabeth got the news that she was queen of England. Now the King's African Rifles had replaced the tourists, and the nightly watch was for men. That's when the Mau Mau came out of the forest to attack.

I asked a major who was showing us some military maps how we could tour the front. "I'll take you there myself," he said, and that afternoon he picked us up in his Land Rover, a rifle laid between the two front seats. I asked him whether we should also be armed. "You should," he said, "but the rule is that everyone can carry a gun except journalists." We drove north along roads that were ideal for ambush. "It's a bit touch-and-go along here," the major said. "You never know when the chaps are going to pop out at you." At Nyeri he took us to see the charred ruins of Treetops, which the Mau Mau had burned down, putting the match, symbolically, to tourism and to the queen who had stayed there. We talked with some soldiers at a watchpost surrounded by a moat with sharp bamboo spears, and then the major dropped us at the Outspan Hotel.

The Outspan was one of those sprawling resort hotels that branch out in long wings, like a game of dominoes in its final stage. A British lady at the front desk took us to our room. We walked and walked—it was at the very end of one of the wings. "I know you'll like it here," she said. "These French doors open over a nice lawn, and there's a fine view of the Aberdare forest." I would have preferred to look out on a moat of sharp bamboo spears. I told the lady we weren't choosy about the view; did she have anything nearer the lobby? She said all the other rooms were reserved for army officers who came from Nairobi with their wives. "Actually, though, they don't come up much anymore. The hotel's almost empty right now."

In the oak-paneled dining room we were almost alone. The only other diners were a few old settlers. I heard one of them talking about "poor Leakey," and I asked if the rumor of his being buried alive was true. "That's only half of it," he said. "We've heard that the Mau Mau priestess said that *two* prominent white people would have to be buried alive. So far there hasn't been a second human sacrifice. But then we don't get many prominent white people out this way anymore—writers and that sort of thing."

We retired for what was to be the longest night of our married life. First we dragged most of the furniture across the room and propped it against the French doors. But every rattle that was probably only the wind might not have been the wind, and long after midnight we were still wide awake. The face I shaved the next morning looked several years older than the one I had shaved 24 hours earlier. By evening we were back in Nairobi, having toured the war zone and talked with some British families who had stuck it out on their isolated farms. Then I holed up in the New Stanley, not far from the room where Hemingway had recently medicated himself with Haig & Haig after the crash of his bush plane, and wrote five Mau Mau articles for the *Herald Tribune*. Then I stopped playing journalist and took my bride to Mombasa, on the coast. We had crossed the continent and deserved a swim in the Indian Ocean.

We got out of Africa by going down the Nile through the Sudan by train and steamer to Aswan and Luxor and Cairo. Where we really said good-bye to colonial Africa was at Khartoum—a stop traceable to my addiction to *The Four Feathers*, the movie that tells with Victorian panache the story of General Kitchener's 1897 expedition to Khartoum to avenge the death of General Gordon and the defeat of his British army by the messianic Mahdi twelve years earlier. In Omdurman, the native city across the river, we visited the Mahdi's house, a small adobe building that had been converted into a museum. It was full of mementos of the victory over the British, displayed in glass cases: weapons, uniforms, medals, flags and other military curios. A steady crowd of Sudanese filed reverently through the rooms.

Khartoum was the city the British built, where two generations of colonial servants had made their desolate lives. It was fiercely hot. The streets were named for Kitchener and other heroes of the empire; one large square had a statue of General Gordon riding a camel. But Britain's long involvement with the Sudan was coming to an end. Unlike Kenya and Uganda, the Anglo-Egyptian Sudan had already set in motion a timetable for the withdrawal of the colonizers. Only in the bookstore did we see English people in any number. They were waiting for the weekly arrival of the *Times* of London. But the plane was late, and white-haired brigadiers and pale wives in flowered hats poked impatiently among old Penguin editions and tried to keep the children amused with picture books.

The next day, at the railroad station, we saw our first actual departures. Half of Khartoum seemed to be taking the train with us, and the other half was there to see it off. Old sheikhs and tribal chiefs squatted on the platform, smoking acrid cigarettes and shouting final words to their sons and cousins jammed into the third-class carriages. A small knot of English colonials had come to say good-bye to a husband and wife who had served in the Sudan for 20 years. The pale-faced English men and women huddled together and sang "Auld Lang Syne" as the couple boarded the train. Caroline and I were leaving a continent of dissolving dreams. In a few more years General Gordon and his camel would be torn down. The Mahdi had won after all.

I first told that story in my first book, *Any Old Place With You*, in 1957. The writing was far more extensive. One entire chapter was devoted to our precarious drive around Ruanda-Urundi. Another described our voyage down the Nile and our stay at Luxor, where we found a Hollywood crew shooting a crowd scene for Cecil B. DeMille's *The Ten Commandments* at Queen Hatshepsut's tomb in the Valley of the Dead. Later chapters described our subsequent trip to Burma, Thailand, Cambodia and Hong Kong. It was an amiable-looking book, with drawings by the *New Yorker* artist Robert Day showing Caroline and me in various comical predicaments, and I was very pleased with it. I thought it was terrific.

I've now read it again, and it's not so terrific. *Any Old Place With You* represented a tradition of travel writing that was about to become unacceptable. A British creation, dating from Victorian times, it was raised to a high gloss by authors like Evelyn Waugh in the 1920s and '30s. Its roots were not in journalism but in humor writing: the lighthearted travel book and the comic novel. Often the two were interchangeable. Typically, Waugh wrote a droll travel book in 1932, *They Were Still Dancing*, about his frustrated efforts to cover the grandiose coronation of Haile Selassie in Abyssinia. A few years later he recycled that experience into the hilarious novel *Scoop*, in which a London newspaper mistakenly sends its nature correspondent to a feudal African country to cover an outlandish war.

In all those books it was the literary convention to treat indigenous people as comic props—quaint folk seemingly put on earth to torment Western writers and tourists with their ineptitude. The writers, in turn, deliberately put themselves in preposterous or dangerous situations at the hands of the "natives." When the American humorist S. J. Perelman took up the genre after World War II, with *Westward Ha!* and *The Swiss Family Perelman*, he subjected himself to flagellations that he took to be requirements of the trade. Later, for a *New Yorker* series on East Africa, he camped out on the veldt with a cantankerous all-girl safari and sailed as deck passage from Mombasa to Zanzibar on a squalid Arab dhow.

Perelman was one of my early addictions, and I was still under his influence when I wrote *Any Old Place With You*. I seem to have felt that my first obligation was to entertain the reader and only secondly to understand and explain the cultures I was writing about. I now see that I had those priorities exactly backward. The following passage from the book—my younger self on a dissecting table—is typical of the attitude and the style. It begins as our plane is about to land at Khartoum. For the previous two pages I have been tiresomely explaining to Caroline the plot of *The Four Feathers* and the reasons why Khartoum was such a magnet for movie buffs like me—things she already knew very well.

Caroline looked out the window. "We're coming down in the middle of the desert," she said. "There's nothing out there but sand."

"That's what they call a mirage," I told her. "It looks like sand, but you're really looking at the city of Khartoum."

"It must be there some place," she said. "Kitchener wouldn't have come all this way for nothing."

The other passengers began to stir.

"See, everybody's getting off here," I said. "People still have an interest in this place."

"Who do you suppose they all are?"

"Historians, scholars, military experts—that sort of thing."

The plane landed and we got out. The air that greeted us was like a blast furnace.

"Nice little climate they've got here," Caroline said.

A section of desert flew in my eye. "Let's get inside and go through customs," I said. We went into a shack at the edge of the field. The customs officer was a lanky

Sudanese in a soldier's uniform and a fez. He had a rifle at his side and he was paring his nails with a sharp sword. He glanced at us with annoyance.

I handed him our passports. He studied them with the curiosity of a stamp collector coming on a rare issue.

"Do you suppose we're the first Americans who ever got off here?" Caroline asked.

"We may be the first people of any kind to get off here," I said. I pointed to the airstrip. Every one of our fellow passengers, after a brief stretch, was hurrying back onto the plane.

"There goes a plane load of historians, scholars and military experts," Caroline said.

"Phlum bloggha!" shouted the customs boy. He seemed pleased to have us at his mercy. He spoke almost no English, but I caught the fact that we must pay an admission fee. I didn't happen to be loaded with Sudanese money, and to illustrate my plight I heaped some East African shillings on his desk. He gave me an evil leer.

"You no pay, I keep passports," he said.

"No keep passports," I said, snatching them out of his hand.

He replied by hoisting his rifle onto the table. He slammed the bolt. . . .

Today I can't imagine subjecting readers to such persiflage: the breezy language, the strenuous reaching for a gag, the racist patronizing of the Sudanese "boy"—why should he be expected to speak English?—and his "evil" pleasure in blocking our way. But the worst thing about this kind of writing is that most of it isn't true. What's true is that we landed at Khartoum, that only a few passengers disembarked, and that we were given a hard time getting through customs. But none of the things Caroline and I "said" got said. We've been reduced to caricatures of irritable tourists, just as the customs inspector has been reduced to a cartoon bureaucrat. I wish I could report that I treated other local people more responsibly in my book. But the British colonials who showed us around Kenya are no less a stereotype than the Sudanese soldier paring his nails with a knife. They all have names like Flagshaw and Grimsley-Harris and are almost identical twits.

When *Any Old Place With You* was published in 1957 it got pleasant reviews. Nobody called it contrived or condescending; it was just another new arrival in a genre that Western readers had long enjoyed. Then, overnight, the genre was extinct. The colonial powers were ousted and indigenous people everywhere were understood to have their own cultural integrity. They were no longer called "natives" and they weren't "picturesque." Travel writers would have to work harder to tell their story. It had been much too easy for much too long.

Since then I've had plenty of chances to try to get it right. The marriage that began with a trek across Africa has been nourished by travel. After our children, Amy and John, were born, Caroline and I found ways to take them with us. One year we rented a house for a month in a small village in Spain.

Another year we rented a house in a small village in Italy. Then it was back to traveling on our own: to Timbuktu to look for a camel caravan, to Yemen and Petra, Bali and Brazil, Turkey and Morocco, Hanoi and Laos, London and Paris and Rome and Sicily and Dubrovnik and the isles of Greece. Those places have never stopped reverberating in our lives: in the books we read and the art we buy, the music we listen to and the movies we see. Some of our favorite movies come from Mali and Burkina Faso.

In the magazine articles that I wrote about those trips I learned to leave my cultural assumptions at home. I now try to catch the intention of every place I write about: to see it for what it is, or for what it's trying to be, not for what *I* might have expected or wanted it to be. Travel writing is not unlike detective work; it depends on the gathering of dozens of small details. My pleasure is to make a narrative arrangement of those details that will tell the reader something he or she didn't know before—something interesting or amusing. But they also have to be details that interest or amuse *me*. Mere observing and reporting isn't enough. You must make a personal connection with the place you're writing about.

Here's an example from one of our trips, a museum-sponsored tour of the Arabian peninsula. The style is personal; the trip I'm describing is *my* trip, not a generic trip. But the main thing about this passage is that it gets the journalistic job done. It brings the news.

"It's hard today to understand the madness for fragrances in the ancient world," Professor David Soren told us as we sailed along the coast of Oman. He said that frankincense, used for mummification by the Egyptians, was the darling of a heavy traffic in spices that went back to the early Phoenicians and flowered during the "culinary golden age" of Augustus, when Roman emperors developed trade routes that brought cinnamon, cloves and other condiments from as far away as China and the Moluccas. "We're on one of those ancient trade routes right now," Soren said, explaining that the frankincense caravans set out from Oman and went up the Arabian peninsula through Yemen to Petra. Many long-forgotten empires grew fat by controlling that aromatic highway.

I had never stopped to wonder what frankincense was or where it might come from, though the word is infinitely resonant, echoing back to my first childhood hearing of the story of the Nativity. The next day, not far from Salalah, the answer was provided. Our bus stopped beside a stand of frankincense trees, and we all got out to examine them. They were scraggly specimens, heavily picked over by camels, as Professor Darrel Frost pointed out, but they had the integrity of all survivors, and we lingered to touch the curling bark and feel the gum and think our childhood thoughts. That night, back on the ship, Frost explained that the bark rolls up in curlicues to act as insulation against water loss. Insulation against camels is evidently less sophisticated. "Camels are very scenic," Frost said, "but ecologically they're just very large goats."

Here's another passage, describing the city of Salvador in the Brazilian province of Bahia, where I had gone to write an article about some of the African origins of American jazz. I cite it here to remind you that every place has a point—some distinctive identifying trait—that the writer owes it to the reader to find. Otherwise why bother to write about it? These two paragraphs isolate the central idea of Salvador.

If you like the feeling of round cobblestones pressing into your instep, if you like streets that go sharply downhill in one block and sharply uphill in the next, if you like to turn a corner and see a sky-blue Baroque church, if you like the singing of caged birds in 250-year-old doorways, Salvador is for you. It has all the elements that constitute "old-world charm" in the lexicon of certain travel writers. But that's not the point; many old-world cities have old-world charm. What caught my attention was that we were in an African city. These were African faces I was seeing—black, strong, handsome.

The people were wearing block-printed fabrics of African design and they walked as if they were hearing African music. Soon I began to hear some of it myself. It came from a boy playing a *berimbau*, a long bow with a gourd attached to it and a wire strung between its two ends. The wire is plucked with a sharp stone, and the player also uses his stomach as a percussion instrument, holding the gourd against it and tightening his muscles to vary the tone. I had rarely seen a simpler instrument, but its jagged rhythms soon get into the bloodstream, especially if one or two other boys are playing a drum, as they usually are.

Here's one more—a passage about the Aegean Sea—that does several kinds of work. The first part provides helpful information about the logisitics and the appeal of a certain kind of cruise. The second part provides resonance, transporting us back to names and words we first encountered in the classrooms of childhood. We can still picture the blackboards at the front of those rooms—and the chalk and the erasers and the maps. Look for resonance when you write about the places in your life. Your readers will bring strong memories of their own to your story and thereby, subconsciously, do some of your work.

Logistically, the cruise was a magic carpet. I was whisked to a dozen classical sites that I couldn't have visited on my own without countless transactions: catching boats and buses, renting cars, clearing customs, toting bags, finding hotel rooms, hiring guides, packing and unpacking, worrying about missed connections. I was painlessly delivered to out-of-the-way places that had always eluded me. I rode the magic carpet shamelessly and watched the ancient world go by. It went by very fast. Whole civilizations rose and fell within the showing of a few lecturer's slides. Cycladians and Minoans, Mycenaeans and Ionians, Athenians and Macedonians, Romans and Christians, Saracens and Seljuks and Ottomans—all came and went. Power was a will-o'-the-wisp, mighty empires

were dust. Words we hadn't heard since school spilled
out of our professors: stoa, architrave, propylaea,
metope. We were told that we could date a Doric temple
by the thickness of the echinus. We heard about the
archaic smile and the *horror vacui*. Long-forgotten
names went galloping by: Vitruvius, Pausanias, Poly-
crates, Pythagoras. I hadn't thought about Pythagoras
since I first tried to square the hypotenuse. Then one
day we docked at Pythagorian, on Samos. Pythagoras,
we learned, was only one of that island's brilliant sons.
Aesop and Anacreon were two others, and that was just
the A's.

But, ultimately, it's people—memorable people—who
make certain places stick in our minds forever. Look for those
people, wherever you go, and tell us how their story inter-
sected with your life. Here are some people in faraway places
whose stories Caroline and I still carry around.

6.

People Along the Way

ONE OF THE MOVIES I reviewed for the *Herald Tribune* in 1955 was a British film called *The Purple Plain*. It starred Gregory Peck as a pilot stationed in Burma during World War II who cracks under the strain of combat and is nursed back to his better nature by a Burmese girl. The girl was played by Win Min Than, a Burmese actress, who brought unusual grace and gentleness to the role. She was also very beautiful; her name meant "brilliant a millionfold."

To promote the film its producers brought Win Min Than to New York, and a press agent asked me if I would have lunch with her at Sardi's. Usually I avoided that kind of meeting; conversations with actors can be as slow as crossing the Sudan by train. But I'm always up for talk of Southeast Asia, and I went to Sardi's and brought Caroline along. Win turned out to be a warm and generous woman, and at the end of lunch she said that if we ever came to Rangoon we should be sure to look her up. I promised that we would and put it out of my mind. So, undoubtedly, did she.

A few months later I asked Caroline where she would like to go on our next vacation. After crossing Africa I think I had in mind something a little simpler—maybe Bermuda. She said, "I'd like to go to Burma." A letter to Win Min Than brought a welcoming reply, and a call to the Burmese consulate informed us that tourist visas were limited to five days. We made a one-month itinerary that would start in Rangoon and then take us to Thailand, Cambodia and Hong Kong.

Those five days gave us an affection for the Burmese people; they seemed to have a born amiability. On our second night Win Min Than invited us to dinner. She was married to an older businessman, and their home was in an affluent neighborhood. All their Burmese friends spoke English and had a bantering sense of humor. After dinner the men stayed downstairs and drank warm Scotch while the wives went upstairs and sat on a huge bed with much merriment and smoked cheroots. Then a Burmese puppet show was presented as a special treat for us. The ornately carved and costumed puppets were held in great deference, and afterward Win's husband took me to watch them being ceremonially undressed. He wanted me to see that the carver had made them human in every detail.

A few days later Win invited us to tea on a terrace next to her garden. This time her special treat was unannounced. An old Burmese woman suddenly appeared in the garden, accompanied by two men who were carefully carrying a heavy basket. There are certain baskets that proclaim by their shape what they were designed to contain. This one said STAND BACK. The woman removed the lid of the basket and an enormous python slithered out and uncoiled itself on the lawn, not far from where we were sitting. The woman then dallied with the python in various ways, at one point placing its head in her mouth. But my mind wasn't on the performance. All I could think was: how is she going to get that thing back in? Win poured more tea and passed more cakes and chatted of this and that. Caroline's eyes were riveted on the python and on the basket, calculating the geometry. The woman was in no hurry to wind things up; the minuet had many variations. Finally she coaxed the python up to the opening of the basket and it slowly glided back in. That was tea in Rangoon.

I've used writing to give myself an interesting life and a continuing education—to see the world. But what I'm always looking for as a writer is someone like Win Min Than who will make a particular place come alive. That notion was probably in my mind in 1956 when Caroline and I were planning our third trip. We wanted to try something entirely different, and a voice from out of nowhere whispered "South Seas." Not only were the islands of the South Pacific a separate geographical entity, unattached to any continent or culture. They also existed powerfully as an idea—the last paradise, calling to every dreamer eager to slip off the coils of civilization. I thought of all the writers who had answered the call and helped to create the myth: Herman Melville and Joseph Conrad, Robert Louis Stevenson and Henry Adams, Jack London and Rupert

Brooke, Pierre Lôti and Somerset Maugham, Charles Nord-hoff and James Norman Hall. I thought of all the Gauguin paintings of Polynesian girls beside a lagoon and all the movies like *Mutiny on the Bounty* and all the plays like *Rain* and all the songs like "Bali Ha'i" and all the "desert island" imagery: trade winds and swaying palms. I also thought of all the white interlopers who had contaminated the dream—explorers, colonials, traders, missionaries, beachcombers—and who were also part of the myth, adding up to . . . what? We had no idea. There were no tourist guides to consult or friends who had been there. Like so many wayfarers before us, we would just have to take off.

In our atlas Tahiti and Samoa were flyspecks in an immensity of ocean, unimaginably far away. The only air service was an occasional seaplane from Fiji; when it put us down in Tahiti it wouldn't be back for two weeks. Altogether, the trip would take eight weeks, and once again I found myself asking George Cornish for an extra month of vacation and promising to write a series of articles. As a journalistic beat the South Seas were off the map; I couldn't remember any *Herald Tribune* correspondent going there since World War II.

Perhaps I caught Cornish on a day when his timing was off. Ordinarily he was the king of temporizers. A cultivated man from Demopolis, Alabama, he presided over the long decline of his impoverished paper, surviving frequent changes of management, by refining the art of diplomatic delay. From morning to night, editors and reporters trooped into his office to plead for more money or more staff or more editorial space, and he listened to them all with exquisite courtesy, jotting down each request on his engagement pad in handwriting so small and faint that it seemed sure to vanish by nightfall. He could make the horticulture editor Jack Johnston feel that he cared as deeply about mulching as he made the music critic Virgil Thomson feel that he cared about Mozart, and they all left his office in a warm glow of accomplishment. Not until they were back at the watercooler did they realize they had been promised nothing. I often knew Cornish to solve a complaint by waiting for the complainant to resign or retire or even die.

Now, hearing that Caroline and I needed two months to roam the South Seas, he probably decided it would be easiest to let me go. He knew I believed in making my own luck, pushing the boundaries of my employment. If he didn't give me Fiji and Tahiti and Samoa today I would be back tomorrow with some other gig. He also knew that the South Seas had a literary tradition that the *Herald Tribune*'s bookish readers would enjoy being reminded of at the breakfast table. If I could bring back some distant echo of Robert Louis Stevenson, some new tale of Captain Bligh or Captain Ahab, his paper would be a little richer, its slow death staved off a little longer.

Grasping for any morsel of travel information, I remembered that the director John Huston had made a trip through the South Seas to look for movie locations, and I wrote to him to ask if he had any advice. We had met in connection with several of his films, most recently at the premiere of *Moby-Dick* in the old whaling town of New Bedford. God knows where my letter caught up with Huston, but he sent a last-minute telegram suggesting that we talk to Don the Beachcomber at his restaurant in Honolulu when our flight stopped over. With that yellow Western Union form as our amulet, we headed for the South Seas.

Don the Beachcomber, whose real or putative name was Don Beach, received us in his faux-Polynesian emporium, enthroned in a lofty wicker chair that seemed to be his office. As he looked at Huston's telegram and began to mention some names, I realized that the vast region we were about to enter was actually a small world, where everyone knew everyone else and a visitor could be steered to the relatively few people he would find it useful to meet. In Fiji we should sail with Trevor Withers on one of his "Blue Lagoon Cruises" to the Yasawa Islands. Near Suva we might want to call on the aviator Harold Gatty, who achieved fame as Wiley Post's navigator on their historic round-the-world flight in 1931. In Samoa we had to stay at Aggie Gray's hotel; everyone in the islands stayed with Aggie. In Tahiti we should look up Sarah Hall, widow of the writer James Norman Hall.

The names had exactly the right ring, and I wrote them all down. We thanked Don for the generous fruits of his beach-combing and slipped out into the fragrant Hawaiian night. My head was already in the islands and I couldn't wait to get there.

The crew of the *Bounty* called at Tahiti in 1788 and stayed five months. Our welcome was no less potent 168 years later when we were deposited in Papeete, Tahiti's capital, by a seaplane of Tasman Empire Airways. Our hotel, Les Tropiques, had a sign that said: THE BAR WILL OPEN EVERY DAY AT 9 A.M. FOR YOUR CONVENIENCE. The French government had recently levied a 30 percent tax on the import of books, but beer was duty-free. The message was clear: if you want to catch up on your reading, do it somewhere else.

Papeete was a patchwork of rickety wooden buildings with corrugated-tin roofs. The main daytime activity was hanging around the waterfront. Every day we would spend a few hours there, seeing what new ships had arrived and listening to tales of the sea; old-timers called it "yarning." South Sea life was so dependent on inter-island trade that the comings and goings of every boat were known and kept track of. Often the yarns took a historical turn, dealing with feats of navigation by skippers who made it through a narrow opening in the reef in rough weather, or who didn't make it. "She's lying off Raiatea now," someone would say, recalling the exact location of the reef and the circumstances of the wreck. Papeete had the folksiness of a New England village, and after only a few days we had made many friends.

I liked hearing the sonorous names of the boats and the islands they had come from: the Nukuhiva from the Marquesas, the Pukapuka from Rarotonga, the Isabelle Rose from the Tuamotus. But the day's catch might also include a luxury yacht from Cannes or a lone pilot sailing around the world. One day Ernest K. Gann, whose action novel *The High and the Mighty* had become a hit movie with Gregory Peck, arrived in his private yawl. He was a rangy, easygoing man, somewhat resembling Peck, and I was delighted to see him turn up: it was the perfect match of voyager and destination. Tahiti was every man's fantasy island, and Gann was that almost-vanished literary type, the author-adventurer, living out the same virile dreams that he wrote for his fictional heroes.

Farther down the beach we found a French explorer named Eric de Bisschop and four other men getting ready to make a 10,000-mile voyage to South America and back on a 40-foot bamboo raft. Famous for an earlier feat of endurance at sea, a two-year journey by catamaran from Hawaii to Marseilles via the Cape of Good Hope in the mid-1930s, De Bisschop was now 65. But there was nothing arthritic about the way he clambered down from his raft, the *Tahiti-Nui*, to greet us. He was a small, wiry man with piercing blue eyes. They were the eyes of a true believer, and I believed they would take him where he wanted to go.

The purpose of his expedition, he told us, was to prove his theory that the islands of Oceania were not settled by the present Polynesians, but by an earlier race of navigators who explored the Pacific around 300 b.c., the same "missing" people who left stone statues on Easter Island, in the Marquesas and on certain islands near Tahiti. De Bisschop told us that he and his crew planned to sail south until they met a westerly wind that he believed those navigators used, at about 35 degrees latitude, one of the least-known oceanic regions of the world. They would follow that wind to Valparaiso, Chile—a distance of 5,000 miles that he estimated would take three to four months. Then they would proceed north along the coast to Callao, Peru, and sail back to Tahiti on the Humboldt and Equatorial currents.

"Anyone can make that return trip," de Bisschop said scornfully, referring to Thor Heyerdahl's much-publicized *Kon-Tiki* raft voyage a decade earlier, which purported to prove that the Polynesians originated in South America, not on the mainland of Asia. "I could drop a piece of wood in the water off Peru and it would come back to Tahiti," he told us. The prevailing view along the Papeete waterfront was that Heyerdahl's theory was based on flimsy evidence and that his voyage didn't prove anything. (Since then it has been generally discredited.) A week later, half of Tahiti came down to the harbor to see the expedition off. Solemn ceremonies were held, a priest blessed the *Tahiti-Nui*, and Polynesian boys in canoes escorted the raft out into the lagoon. It looked like a small home for five men going 10,000 miles. We watched until the raft bobbed through a passage in the reef and its sail filled with the winds of the Pacific Ocean. Soon it was out of sight.

Eric de Bisschop personified much that I went to the South Seas to look for. I can still see those blue eyes and still see his raft getting smaller and smaller and finally dropping off the face of the earth. When I got back to New York I kept watch in the newspapers for some word of his expedition. Finally I saw the item I was waiting for. Six and a half months after leaving Papeete, it said, the *Tahiti-Nui* was shipwrecked by a severe storm near the Juan Fernández Islands, off the coast of Chile. De Bisschop and his crew were rescued by a Chilean freighter. They had fallen just short of their goal but had proved their theory about that early race of navigators and the westerly wind they could have used. De Bisschop himself died on the return voyage when his raft foundered on a reef in the Cook Islands.

James Norman Hall was the most popular American who ever lived in Tahiti; his funeral in 1951, five years before our visit, was still warmly remembered. Hall, who was from a small farming town in Iowa, first came to Tahiti in 1920 to write a book about the South Seas with Charles Nordhoff. Both men had been aviators with the Lafayette Escadrille, the glamorous corps of volunteer American pilots attached to the French army in World War I. They became friends when they were brought together afterward to write the squadron's official history.

The event that would shape Hall's life occurred in 1916 when he was a student pilot at the Blériot school of aviation near Versailles. One day the class was excused because of bad weather and Hall went to Paris to hunt for a volume of poetry. In the bookstore his eye was caught by an 1831 volume called *The Mutiny on the Bounty* by Sir John Barrow, secretary of the British Admiralty. It was a factual account of Captain Bligh's voyage to Tahiti to bring a cargo of young breadfruit trees to the West Indies and of the subsequent shipboard mutiny. Hall was so taken by the book that he bought it and kept it with his wartime possessions.

By the late 1920s both Hall and Nordhoff had married and built homes on Tahiti and written several books on their own. But the dismal truth, they admitted to each other one day, was that their literary careers were stalled; maybe it was time to collaborate again. Hall asked Nordhoff whether he had ever heard of the *Bounty* mutiny. Nordhoff said that of course he had, but that surely many books about it had been written. Hall said he had never seen anything except Barrow's book. Nordhoff said he wished he could get a copy of that book. Hall went to a shelf and got it down.

Nordhoff read it overnight and came back, Hall remembered, "in a dither." He said it was the perfect story for their combined talents. Hall pointed out that it was actually three stories: the mutiny itself, Bligh's 3,000-mile voyage with 18 sailors in an open boat, and the adventures of Fletcher Christian and his fellow mutineers on Pitcairn Island. After confirming that the saga had indeed lain untouched by writers for more than a century, the two men wrote the trilogy—*Mutiny on the Bounty*, *Men Against the Sea* and *Pitcairn Island*—that became one of the smash hits of commercial publishing in the 1930s. It also spawned one of the memorable movies of that era, with Charles Laughton as Bligh and Clark Gable as Fletcher Christian in two of their best roles.

Caroline and I went around to see Hall's widow at the house she and Hall built in the Arue district of Tahiti, ten miles outside town. It was a rambling wooden house with screened verandas, surrounded by bright tropical foliage. Sarah Hall was a person of unusual gaiety. A handsome woman with amused blue eyes, she was the daughter of an English sea captain and was one-sixteenth Polynesian, her Tahitian great-grandmother having married an English sea captain named Richmond. But French was the language of her girlhood, and she spoke English with an accent so piquant that Hall refused to teach her how to correct it.

Hall was very much alive in the house, his hat still hanging on a peg in the vestibule, his thousands of books stuffed into bookshelves that spilled into the kitchen. But the books that caught my eye were the ones he had used for research, which he kept in the room where he did his writing. The room was exactly as he left it: an ink-stained blotter on the desk, a wobbly chair behind it, an old typewriter on a nearby table and a falling-apart atlas within easy reach. Stretching across one bookshelf were 27 volumes by Joseph Conrad, who was his hero and for whom he named his son. (Conrad Hall would make his own name as a Hollywood cinematographer, winner of an Academy Award for *Butch Cassidy and the Sundance Kid*.) Hall's copy of *Lord Jim* had been thumbed almost to pieces. "He had read it so many times," Sarah Hall said, "that I once asked him, 'Haven't you memorized it by now?'"

Keeping Conrad company were the complete works of Robert Louis Stevenson, the 12-volume *Works of Benjamin Franklin*, the nine-volume *Writings of Thomas Jefferson*, and sets of Washington Irving, Thoreau, Emerson, Hawthorne, Mark Twain, Thackeray and Sir Walter Scott. Modern American literature was broadly represented: Thurber, Steinbeck, Sinclair Lewis, Sarah Orne Jewett and the writer Hall most admired, Willa Cather. One entire wall was occupied by books of naval history: *The Life of Admiral Bligh*; *Trial of the Bounty Mutineers*; *Sea Life in Nelson's Time*, by John Masefield; *English Seamen*, by Robert Southey; 12 old books of *Naval Chronicles*; 69 volumes of the *Annual Register* of England from 1758 to 1827, and dozens of other volumes, many with place markings sticking out and notes scribbled in the margins.

"I was always jealous of the books—they took so much of my husband's time," Sarah Hall said. "He once asked me what I wanted to do with them after he died—maybe give them to a library? I said, 'Why, Jimmy, it wouldn't be my house if it didn't have those books.'"

The house also revealed Hall as a sentimental man. Photographs of his family and friends and his companions in the Lafayette Escadrille were everywhere. Not on view were his many medals, including the *Croix de Guerre*, the *Légion d'honneur* and the Purple Heart, or his aviation mementos, such as the pocket calendar he carried as a prisoner of war in Germany.

"I'd like to have those medals out," Sarah Hall said. "But Jimmy wouldn't approve of that."

Hall is buried on a hill behind the house. His grave looks down on the brilliant blue bay where Samuel Wallis discovered Tahiti, where Captain Cook came to observe the transit of Venus on his first voyage, and where Bligh's Bounty dropped anchor—a view rich in the history that Hall brought to life for countless readers. His epitaph is from one of his early poems:

Look to the northward, stranger,
Just over the hillside there.
Have you in all your travels seen
A land more passing fair?

If James Norman Hall is very much alive in those paragraphs, Robert Louis Stevenson was no less alive when we got to Apia, in Western Samoa. (We did stay with Aggie Gray at her hotel for three weeks.) Stevenson's house, Vailima, a white frame building with a blue roof, several verandas and broad views down to the Pacific, was the one where he and his extended family spent the last four years of his life and where he died in 1890 at the age of forty-four. The Samoans called him "Tusitala," teller of tales, and some of them believed that his ghost lived in the house. But I only felt serene vibrations there. So did the New Zealand high commissioner, G. R. Powles, whose official residence it now was.

"Mrs. Powles and I have lived here for eight years," he told us, "and we're alone at night—the servants sleep out. But never once have I snapped awake in the dark and thought, 'What was that?' as you do in so many houses." I couldn't help thinking of all the boys who stayed up late reading *Treasure Island* and *Kidnapped* and *Dr. Jekyll and Mr. Hyde* and later snapped awake thinking "What was that?"

I mention the aliveness of Hall and Stevenson to remind you not to overlook the dead when you travel as a writer in search of interesting people. They are often strongly present in the place where they lived. With luck you can still find a relative or a widow, as we found Sarah Hall in Tahiti, or a custodian of memory, like G. R. Powles in Samoa. You can also find artifacts of the life you want to reconstruct: a hat hanging on a peg, an old typewriter, a book with a place mark still sticking out ("What was he looking for on *that* page?").

Ideally, however, I want the men and women I meet in my travels to be alive in their historic moment—which is also my historic moment. Here's a final snapshot from our album. The time is exactly 40 years later—1996—and the place is Hanoi. Caroline and I had stopped off there on our way to Laos, where I would finally be indulging an old yen to visit the royal capital of Luang Prabang. Hanoi had only recently begun to welcome western tourists, and we didn't know what to expect.

The city charmed us with its energy. Under their umbrella of trees the streets were a river of humanity—people on foot, on bicycles, on mopeds and in pedicabs, all moving at high speed. In the old quarter of Hanoi we were struck by the beauty of the men and women going about the day's tasks: buying and selling, cooking meals on the sidewalk, looking after their children. That these gentle people had been our reviled enemy for so many years seemed outlandish.

We had been given the name of Duong Tuong Tran, Vietnam's most influential art critic and one of its broadest intellectuals—a writer and poet and a translator of American and Russian literature into Vietnamese. His gallery was a gathering place for artists, writers, musicians, dancers and filmmakers. I telephoned the gallery to ask Duong Tuong if we could call on him. He said he would be glad to see us. We squeezed into a narrow pedicab and were wheeled through the streets. Finally the driver stopped at a building so small and nondescript that we thought he had brought us to the wrong address. But the driver pointed to a small sign with an arrow that said THE MAI GALLERY. We followed the arrow down an alley to a building in the rear that was only slightly larger. It didn't look as if it could hold many artists, writers, musicians, dancers and filmmakers.

Inside, however, the gallery was thick with people. They were looking at paintings on the walls and rummaging through pictures in drawers and talking about art. Duong

Tuong's grown son and daughter introduced themselves to us, and after a while their father came in from another room, where he had been showing someone a painting. He was a compact man with black hair and thick horn-rimmed glasses, somewhat bent over, looking at least as old as his 63 years. He had a scholar's face: intelligent and quizzical. He led us to a low table in the corner, his wife brought tea, and the four of us sat down to talk.

The other guest at the table was the Vietnam War. Nobody had mentioned it during our stay in Hanoi, and nobody mentioned it now, but I couldn't push it out of my mind. "Hanoi" had been a political word for so long that I had never thought of it as a place I might actually visit and feel an affinity for. Yet here we were in an art gallery in Hanoi, talking with a Vietnamese man of my generation whose life had been devoted to the same concerns: writing and culture and the arts. Was the war really behind us at last?

Duong Tuong told us that Hanoi then had more than 60 art galleries. The artists, he said, are doing good and innovative work, some looking to Europe as their influence, others following their own vision. He himself had just come back from a trip to the United States to refresh his own knowledge. He had particularly liked the Mondrian show at the Museum of Modern Art and the Vermeer exhibit at the National Gallery in Washington.

More tea was brought, and we chatted about the art scene in Hanoi and New York, the conversation stopping and starting up again, a fragile vessel kept afloat by the love of art that was our only point of contact.

Duong Tuong mentioned that during his visit to Washington he had visited the Vietnam Memorial. Here it comes, I thought. He said he was interested to learn that its designer, Maya Lin, was a Chinese-American woman. We told him we happened to know Maya Lin. Our son, John, a New York painter himself, knew her at Yale, and I had interviewed her for an article about her civil rights memorial in Montgomery, Alabama. That seemed to ease the situation.

"When I was at the Vietnam Memorial," Duong Tuong said, "I wrote a poem and left it there at the wall. Would you like to see it?"

We said we would very much like to see it. He got up and went to a desk and brought back the poem, which was typed on a piece of paper, and handed it to Caroline. She looked at it for a long time. She had tears in her eyes and couldn't say anything. Then she gave it to me, and I couldn't say anything either.

Finally I managed to ask Duong Tuong if we could keep the poem and if he would inscribe it for us, and he did. It said:

At the Vietnam Wall

because i never knew you
nor did you me
     i come

because you left behind mother,
    father and betrothed
and i wife and children
     i come

because love is stronger than enmity
and can bridge oceans
>   i come

because you never return
and i do
>   i come

>   DUONG TUONG *Washington, D.C., Nov. 21, 1995*

7.

The Uses of Memory

MY BOOK *Spring Training* was born, though I didn't know it at the time, in 1982, in Winter Haven, Florida, at the spring training camp of the Boston Red Sox. I was sitting in the grandstand in a sea of codgers, codging the time away. The sun was warm, the grass was green, and the air was alive with the sounds of rebirth: bat meeting ball, ball meeting glove, players and coaches chattering across the diamond. They were sounds that hadn't been heard in the land since the World Series ended in October.

I was a pilgrim on an old American pilgrimage. Every winter since the 1920s, families from all over the United States have journeyed to Florida—and, more recently, to the Southwest—to watch their favorite baseball teams get in shape for the season and to look over the new crop of rookies. I grew up on the names of those Florida towns. Lakeland!

Vero Beach! Clearwater! Bradenton! Of all the romantic datelines in the newspapers of my boyhood—the *New York Herald Tribune*, the *New York Times* and the baseball-obsessed *New York Sun*—none sent as strong a message as those towns in the "Grapefruit League" that annually came out of hibernation. To every fan stuck in the frozen North they shouted the good news: the long freeze is over.

To be a codger it is only necessary to have a brain crammed with baseball memories, and I had several generations' worth, going back to my boyhood team, the New York Giants of Carl Hubbell, Bill Terry and Mel Ott. Much of my youth was spent—and by no means misspent—in the longitudinal Polo Grounds, a rickety structure of dark green wood. It made me forever partial to ballparks that weren't prisoners of symmetry, like Boston's Fenway Park and Brooklyn's Ebbets Field, which were laid out in obedience to existing street patterns. Bedford Avenue, which ran behind the right-field fence of Ebbets Field, was entwined with the lives of fans listening to Dodgers games on the radio. "There's a long drive to right field and it's . . . it's . . . in Bedford Avenue!" was the best or worst of sentences.

From the moment I got to Winter Haven the omens were right. The Red Sox ballpark had the same relaxed charm as its dowager mother in Boston. Jim Rice was doing stretching exercises along the third-base line, almost near enough to touch. Carl Yastrzemski was talking with two fans at the railing. Johnny Pesky, long retired as a Boston shortstop and now a coach, was playing pepper with Dwight Evans. Other coaches were hitting fungoes eternally into the Florida sky. Winter Haven indeed! Winter Heaven was more like it.

I bought a hot dog and a beer and took a seat in the stands. A rookie left-hander was on the mound, warming up for an intrasquad game. I was enjoying his form, wondering if this was his season to make it to the big leagues. I told the man next to me that the young pitcher reminded me of Warren Spahn. The man said he thought he looked like Preacher Roe. His wife said the kid was a ringer for Harvey Haddix. An old codger mentioned Lefty Grove. A young codger mentioned Vida Blue. We were typical springtime fools, seeing what we wanted to see.

ℂ What you are reading is the first chapter of my book *Spring Training*. Notice how many different kinds of introductory work the chapter does. It's reportorial: it establishes a specific time and place. It's also personal: it establishes the writer's identity. All writing is a journey, and it begins with an invitation. This chapter is a mini-memoir of one piece of my life: all the hours I've spent playing and following baseball. Readers know at the start of the trip what sort of person their tour guide is: why I decided to write the book, what I know about the game, and what psychological baggage I'll be bringing along.

You must be equally forthcoming. If you're writing about some special interest of yours—cars or boats, horses or dogs, gardening or fishing, music or dance—let us know at the outset how the fever first struck you and how it continues to rule your life. We are all odd ducks in our hobbies and our obsessions, and human oddity is interesting. What's interesting is not necessarily the hobby itself. If you were to write a purely factual book about "fishing" we would soon be nodding off; that's what encyclopedias are for. Your subject is the transaction between yourself and fishing—as a sport, as a pastime, as therapy, as a buddy experience, as a solitary experience, as a nature experience, as a spiritual experience, as a food-gathering experience, or whatever drew you to it. Trust your obsession to be your best calling card. Tell us about it. ❡

The game began. Nobody cared who won; that wasn't the point. The point was to train and to teach—to get the club tuned for the long season ahead. I thought of how often the sportswriter Red Smith reminded us that baseball is a game that little boys play. That truism would never be truer than in spring training. Soon enough the media would age these boys beyond their years by harping on their contracts and their agents, their sulks and their scrapes and their sore arms. But for six weeks in February and March they were allowed to be what they were: young men who played a wonderful game wonderfully well.

Even the Red Sox manager, Ralph Houk, looked human. I saw no sign of the tormented soul that every manager becomes when the season begins, prowling the dugout and popping Rolaids to calm the furies in his stomach. Several codgers remembered how tough Houk was when he came up to the Yankees in 1947. Now they called to the "Iron Major" and asked if he was going to bring Boston a pennant this year. He ambled over to the railing and chatted with them about the team and its chances; he was everybody's next-door neighbor, talking about his lawn and his power tools. Spring training had turned even the Iron Major to some softer metal.

So the afternoon slipped by in contentment. The ancient rhythms and continuities of the game were intact; we could have been watching a game in 1882, not 1982. No organist toyed with our emotions, no electronic scoreboard told us when to cheer. We were suspended in a unique pocket of time, unlike any other season in baseball's long year. It was a time of renewal for the players and also for the fans. It was a time for looking both forward and back: forward to the new season and as far back as the oldest codger could recall. And what made it all work was memory. Memory was the glue that held baseball together as the continuing American epic.

℀ If this chapter has a high emotional content, it's because it does more than you think it's going to do. At first it's just an account of a particular moment in a particular place: an afternoon at a ballpark in a small town in Florida. But it takes a turn when the codgers begin to recall old ballplayers they once saw play, going back to Lefty Grove in the 1930s. At that point it moves beyond Florida and becomes a piece about America—about an American ritual so minutely preserved in statistics and anecdotal lore that it connects people of all ages who watch a game on any given day. And the glue that holds them together is memory. The piece, finally, is about memory. That's the *idea* of the piece.

When you write about your own life, much of your

writing will be about a place. You must give us a picture of what the place looked like and felt like: pure description. But why does it still stick in your mind? It sticks because it embodies an idea that's larger than the place itself. Try to find that idea. When nonfiction is raised to an art, it's usually because the writer imposed on the facts an organizing shape or notion—an *idea*—that hadn't been attached to them before.

I think of Tom Wolfe's book *The Right Stuff*, an account of the astronauts who pioneered America's space program. Wolfe's reporting throughout is solid; he hasn't embellished the facts. The value he adds is to attribute the astronauts' success to certain traits of character that he analyzes and defines as "the right stuff." That raises his book to an art, lifts it above other books about the space program, and gives us an intellectual mechanism for pondering what it takes to be an explorer and to leave the known world behind—a mystery as old as the Phoenicians. Beyond all that, Wolfe's postulation is enjoyable. It's fun to tag along on his ride.

I'm not claiming to be a philosopher for extracting the nugget of memory from the common soil of spring training. It's there for any writer to see. Tell your story plainly and its deeper truths will emerge. In this opening chapter I began by just describing what I saw and heard at the Red Sox camp: pure reporting. Only when I stopped to think about what the codgers in the grandstand were really saying—that the rookie left-hander we were watching was every left-hander who had ever come to spring training—did I see that my real subject was memory. "Memory" is one of the most powerful words that writers are given. I only had to mention memory and readers would bring their own associations to my piece, taking it to corners of their life I couldn't begin to imagine. I was also nudged down memory trails of my own. Read on. ℭ

In 1988 an editor asked me if I had ever thought of writing a book about baseball. I never had; my baseball writing consisted mainly of childhood memoirs. Nor was I sure that baseball needed another book—it was hardly a threatened species. Writing about baseball seemed to be a validating rite for the American male; no game is more deeply connected to the American psyche. Psychiatrists would say that we write about baseball to cling to our youth and to stay plugged in to the long stream of collective lore. As therapy, however, it has its risks; the classics of the literature—Ring Lardner's *You Know Me Al*, Mark Harris's *Bang the Drum Slowly*, Roger Kahn's *The Boys of Summer*—are tinged with sadness and loss. The reality of baseball is finally no different from anybody else's reality. Even the boys of summer grow old.

Still, I liked the idea of writing a whole book about baseball—combining my vocation and my addiction. But was any subject left? I rummaged in my memory grooves to see what images might turn up. I thought of all the summer evenings of my boyhood when I switched my Philco radio to WOR at seven o'clock—the family dinner had to wait—to get the ball scores from Stan Lomax. Lomax's headlong voice conveyed more information in 15 minutes than most people could in an hour. I thought of all the candy-and-cigar stores where I tried to track down the few cards that were still missing from my Big League Gum collection. The name of the cigar, in ornate script, formed a stained-glass panel in the store window, calling me on. *Optimo! La Primadora! Garcia Grande!* I thought of the thousands of hours I spent playing a mechanical baseball game with my friend Charlie Willis, keeping complete box scores for our respective teams.

I thought of all the games I tried to organize—a Charlie Brown ever hopeful of finding enough players to form two teams—and of all the games I played alone against the side of our house with a tennis ball, impersonating all 18 players on two major-league clubs. If my parents had only looked out the window they could have seen Ted Williams. I thought of my only home run; it came back unannounced and previously unremembered from my army days in World War II—a low line drive that skipped past the right-fielder and rolled down a hill in Naples, giving me time to round the bases. I thought of all the ballparks I had sat in, all the games I had heard on the radio, all the games I had stayed up to watch after everyone else had gone to bed.

But one memory that came back insistently was of the day I spent at the Red Sox camp in Winter Haven. Much of what I loved about the game was compressed into that afternoon. Had a book ever been written about spring training? I couldn't think of one. I liked the fact that it was a time of teaching and learning; I was a teacher myself. I also liked the fact that the fans and the players could still be part of each other's lives. Nowhere would that sense of shared values—of baseball as a common American possession—be more palpable than in a Florida spring training town.

I decided to go in search of that once-a-year relationship between one major-league team and its wintertime town.

But which team? And which town? That was the crucial decision that would shape the book.

How did I make that decision? I'll take you through the process; I think it will help you to arrive at the same kinds of decisions when you write about your own life. Organizing a long project is the most underestimated task in nonfiction writing. You must relentlessly distill and condense. Herman Melville couldn't write a book about "whaling." He had to write about one man and one whale. Jane Austen couldn't write a book about "pride and prejudice." She wrote about one man and one woman contending with pride and prejudice. I couldn't write a book about "baseball." I had to make a series of reducing decisions.

First, I reduced the huge subject of baseball to one six-week period. Historically, it was a period devoted to just one activity: teaching and learning. That would be my subject.

Next, I decided not to visit the spring training camps of all the major-league clubs. I would write about *one* club that trained in *one* town. That would give my book its American context. The book would be grounded in an authentic

American place and its annual role as host to a group of athletes from another part of the country.

I knew I wanted a team from the American heartland—one that had a long history in its city and its region. That ruled out all the newer "expansion" clubs and all the franchises that have moved from one city to another—as the Braves, for example, migrated from Boston to Milwaukee to Atlanta. I also wanted a team that trained in Florida, where clubs have trained since the 1920s. That ruled out all the teams that later began to train in Arizona.

I didn't want to write about the Boston Red Sox, much as I had enjoyed my afternoon in Winter Haven. They were too eastern, too patrician, too white. They were also too written-about—the favorite choice of authors who find some kind of epiphany in rooting for a team that will always let them down. Self-flagellation is not one of the things I bring to the ballpark.

My ideal choice was the St. Louis Cardinals because they are an old Mississippi River club. The Mississippi is one of America's central myths, the others being Abraham Lincoln, the Civil War, the American West, and baseball; writers who can get two myths for the price of one are ahead before they start. But the Cardinals trained in St. Petersburg, a city they had long shared with other teams. I wanted no divided affections between the town and its adopted club.

Detroit was a good possibility. I've always liked the Tigers, and they trained in Lakeland, another small Florida town that comes alive every spring with the arrival of its northern sons. But I was a National League fan; mine was the older and purer league, scornful of such adulterants as the designated hitter. The Philadelphia Phillies? A fine old club, but they trained in Clearwater, and Clearwater was a Gulf Coast town; its heart was on the beach and out on the water. The Cincinnati Reds? Another historic old club, but they had just moved to a new training camp in a place called Plant City. Plant City?

Who was left? I went back to my list. The Pittsburgh Pirates, a 98-year-old club. They trained in Bradenton. That rang some bells. Bradenton and I went back a long way. Major-league clubs had trained in Bradenton as long as I had been following baseball—since Dizzy Dean's Cardinals, the rowdy "Gas House Gang"—and probably longer. As far as I knew, it had no other identity, unlike its upscale neighbor, Sarasota, which has museums and other cultural shrines.

I called a former Yale student of mine who grew up in Bradenton and asked him about the town. He told me that the Pirates had trained there for 20 years; that McKechnie Field was the most old-timey of all the spring ballparks; that the town had an active Pirates Boosters Club; that Dizzy Dean once owned a gas station there, and that Edd Roush, the oldest living member of the Baseball Hall of Fame, had been a winter resident since 1952.

I had only one more question: where exactly was McKechnie Field? Several major-league clubs had recently built sophisticated training "facilities" in places that weren't near anything. The Mets had just opened a complex near Port St. Lucie, on Florida's other coast, choosing a site so far from human habitation that it still had no access roads or lodgings.

"McKechnie Field is right in town," my student said.

"What kind of street is it on?" I asked.

"It's your kind of street," he said. "It's got auto-body shops." He remembered my penchant for authentic American detail.

"Say no more," I said. Bradenton sounded ideal—and so, I realized, did the Pirates. All kinds of memories tumbled into place. The Pirates had been my favorite National League team, after the Giants, when I was growing up; I always tried to get to the Polo Grounds when the "Bucs" were in town. I liked to watch Honus Wagner rapping out grounders for infield practice. The greatest shortstop of all time, who had played his entire career with the Pirates, from 1900 to 1917, was then a Pirate coach. Old age had made him so bowlegged that I could hardly picture him as the greatest shortstop of all time. But I took it on faith. Honus was my link to the gods on Mount Olympus.

I called the Pirates to get permission to write about the team, and in February I flew to Bradenton. There, all my reducing decisions put me in a situation that exactly suited my needs. The scale of my book was small and manageable, almost intimate. I didn't feel the anxiety that paralyzes so many writers starting on a project that has ballooned out of control. (Terror reduction is one of my goals as a writing teacher.) McKechnie Field was a preservationist's jewel, partly because the men and women of the Pirates Boosters Club raised enough money every spring by selling programs and renting seat cushions to keep it from falling apart. They became an organic part of my book. I even got to interview Edd Roush, six days before he died at the age of 94. Sitting straight up in a chair in his living room, staring fiercely into the past with vigilant blue eyes, the man who hit over .300 twelve times told me what it was like to play for John McGraw as a rookie in 1916. Nobody else could have anchored my book so far back in baseball's collective memory.

You must make the same kind of reducing decisions when you embark on a project that's large and unwieldy. If you're writing a memoir, choose one narrative that tells a coherent story and discard everything else. A memoir doesn't try to be comprehensive; it's only a slice of one person's life or one family's life. Frank McCourt's *Angela's Ashes* ends when he finally escapes from the slums of Limerick and arrives in America as a teenager. We don't want to know what happened to him in the new country; we've spent all our reader energy just getting him here. McCourt saved the next installment of his life for his next memoir, *'Tis.* Jill Ker Conway's *The Road from Coorain* ends when she escapes from the stifling Australia of her girlhood and gets on the plane to America, where, among other accomplishments, she would become president of Smith College. But those adult years would have a different flavor, and Conway saved them for subsequent memoirs.

If your project is a family history, the size of the task will look daunting. But many reducing decisions can be made. One common problem is whether to write about your mother's or your father's side of the family. Each side had vibrant men and women whose story you would like to preserve. But you can't write about both; they won't fit in the same box. Choose one family and find its central narrative. Tell that story at whatever length feels comfortable; don't try to be definitive. *Then* tackle the other side of the family. Make it a whole other project.

Siblings and relatives can also be reduced out of the process. You're under no obligation to ask all your brothers and sisters and cousins how *they* remember the family saga. They will all remember it differently; there's no one authorized version of the shared past. But you should interview relatives who have a special angle of vision into a family situation—an insight or an anecdote that solves a mystery or fills a hole in the narrative. Finally, however, it's *your* project; you're the one doing all the digging through old records and photographs and letters and diaries. Write what you want to write and leave out the rest. Reduce!

Don't ask: "What will my sister think?" You're bound to feel the censoring eye of your relatives looking over your shoulder, especially if you reveal some family traits that were less than lovable. This fear of family disapproval keeps many family histories from getting written at all. But almost every family wants—and deserves—to have some kind of record left behind of its effort to be a family. If your sister has a problem with your version of the story, she can write her own version. Each will have its own integrity. The integrity of the product should be your goal. Writing about your past is not the medium for settling old grudges and for bashing the elders who didn't understand you. Treat the past and its participants with fairness and respect.

POSTSCRIPT.

At the Pirates' spring training camp the Pittsburgh manager Jim Leyland and his coaches kept reminding me that baseball is a negative game. A batter who hits .300—the game's standard of excellence—fails seven times out of ten. A pitcher who pitches well is often sabotaged by forces he can't control: errors, bad bounces, another pitcher pitching an even better game.

As I listened every day to this litany of failure it took on a familiar ring, and suddenly I realized why. *Writing* is a negative game. Very few sentences come out right the first time, or even the second or third time. Even the best writers are initially .300 hitters, struggling against heavy odds to say what they want to say.

I wondered how the Pirate coaches kept their players "up" for such a long season in the face of such adversity. Positive thinking, I soon saw, was at the heart of everything they said and did. "I refuse ever to be negative," the pitching coach Ray Miller told me. "If you have any negative base in your mind, the negative thing will happen. If you're a pitcher standing on the mound with a man on second and you say, 'That guy's going to score,' he'll score. It's amazing."

During that winter of 1988 I was also teaching writing once a week at a high school in New York. After class I would collect my student papers and catch the plane to Bradenton and spend a few more days at Jim Leyland's optimism academy. When I next met my class I was always struck by how much those Pirate coaches had taught me about how to teach writing to teenagers—matters of confidence and self-esteem.

One of Ray Miller's rituals was one that I had never heard

of. Every time one of his pitchers makes his first major-league start, Miller goes to the bullpen and walks him in to the mound. "The biggest part of my job," he told me, "is to make every kid believe he can perform in front of a lot of people without falling apart."

My book was published the following winter, to coincide with the new spring training season, and I flew to Bradenton one last time to promote it and to autograph copies at McKechnie Field. One afternoon, when the Pirates were playing the Toronto Blue Jays, I was told that it had been arranged for me to throw out the first ball. Me? Throw out the first ball! I've known some minor dreams of glory: I've been in a Woody Allen movie and a "Blondie" comic strip and a lot of double-crostic puzzles. But this was a major dream.

I thought back to the final chapter of my book, which takes place on opening day of the Pirates' regular season, at Three Rivers Stadium in Pittsburgh—the day when spring training finally ends. I describe the pregame ceremonies, including the appearance of Fred Rogers, a Pittsburgh son whose *Mister Rogers' Neighborhood* was then in its 20th year on public television, to throw out the first ball. Rogers made a terrible pitch that had to be blocked in the dirt by the catcher, and I remember thinking, "What a wimp! Anybody can throw a ball that far."

Now I was the one being handed a major-league baseball and led toward the diamond. Suddenly the pitcher's mound looked a long way off. As I walked through the gate I felt an arm around my shoulder and heard a voice saying, "Let me show you how to do this." It was Ray Miller. If there was anybody I wanted to have show me how to throw a baseball it was Ray Miller.

"What you do," he said, "is you don't go all the way out to the mound. You walk down the first-base line, and when you get halfway to first base you turn around and throw to the catcher."

I headed down the first-base line and heard my name and the title of my book being announced over the public-address system. Halfway down the line I turned and saw the Pirate catcher, Junior Ortiz, standing expectantly at the plate, caparisoned in his protective gear and mask, his mitt outstretched. He looked as if he could handle anything I threw at him.

I wound up and pitched the ball toward Ortiz's mitt. I don't remember whether my pitch was high or low or wide, but I do remember that it reached him and didn't bounce in the dirt. Ray Miller had wanted to spare me that possible humiliation.

8.

An Academic Life

I WAS ONCE INVITED by Ohio Wesleyan University to be a teacher-in-residence for two weeks. The prospect appealed to me; I like Ohio's small liberal arts colleges, and the duties sounded satisfying. Only one condition remained, and I put it to the professor on the other end of the phone.

"I'll come," I said, "if I don't have to stay in the college guest house."

There was a pause. The professor asked what kind of lodging I had in mind. "Does the town have anything like a Holiday Inn?" I asked. There was another pause. Finally he said the town did have a Holiday Inn, within walking distance of the college, where I could be put up. I told him that would be fine, and it was; my stay was enjoyable. I was able to be a visitor in academia and still live like a real person, my survival needs provided for.

The campus was mercifully bisected by the main street of the town of Delaware, and I quickly fell into the rhythm of both worlds, starting with breakfast at the generic coffee shop downtown—one of my favorite American institutions—where the talk is of crops and tractors and the men never take off their hats. Best of all, I knew that when I went back to the Holiday Inn to rest I would find one of the most beautiful sights that a traveler on the college circuit can behold: a row of vending machines full of Coca-Colas, potato chips and candy bars.

For want of such infusions of sugar and salt and protein many a visiting lecturer has come close to despair. Nowhere am I so assailed by self-pity as in a college guest house. Lying awake at 2 A.M., unable to sleep because of the mattress, unable to read because of the reading lamp, unable to watch TV because of the absence of a TV, I wonder whether anyone will remember me or find me in the morning. For the guest house isn't always easy to find. At one college, in Illinois, my host drove in widening circles through the night ("It's here someplace") looking for the Baxter Guest House, which the late Buz and Trish Baxter left to their alma mater. The cottage, when we finally found it, appeared to be in deep forest. I could see a pale yellow glow in an upstairs window that I didn't have to be told was the reading lamp on my bedside table.

"Mrs. Hatch, the caretaker, will be around to make you breakfast in the morning," my host said, hurrying away to his own brightly lit home and its larder of beer and Fritos. The mention of Mrs. Hatch brought back a memory of the admiral's widow at the quaint college town in Maryland at whose historic house, over my strenuous protests, I was lodged. "Everyone stays here," my host said, rapping the brass 19th-century door knocker to have me let in. "Mrs. Dobbins has the most wonderful sea stories that she tells at the breakfast table."

Those two nights—and subsequent mornings—were the next-to-last straw. The last straw was the night I spent at Oakland University, near Detroit, which was holding a writers' conference. The college, a 1960s creation, occupied a large estate bequeathed to it by Matilda Dodge Wilson, the widow of an automobile magnate, and her second husband, Alfred Wilson, along with their 110-room home, Meadow Brook Hall. The pleasure of staying at Meadow Brook Hall had been cited by my host as a special inducement for my agreeing to give the keynote speech. My talk was scheduled for Saturday noon, and I duly arrived in time for the participants' Friday night dinner.

Meadow Brook Hall was one of those Tudor mansions that America's industrial barons strewed across the land in the 1920s, clothing their European pretensions in turrets and casement windows, and as soon as I arrived my host said, "We've got a treat for you—you'll be staying in Mr. Wilson's bedroom!" I was led up an ornate winding stairway to the second floor, which branched off into two long corridors of bedrooms, in the style of a resort hotel. Mr. Wilson's enormous bedroom adjoined the even larger bedroom of his wife. The two rooms were connected by an open door with a velvet rope of the kind that excludes the public at a museum. Through the door I could see that Matilda Wilson's room had been left intact, every ladylike accoutrement still in place, her comb and brush still laid out on the dresser.

Dinner was held in a vaulted hall adorned with suits of armor and heraldic shields, and at 9:30, captives of the academic clock, we were all sent up to bed. There was nowhere else to go and nothing else to do. Falling into an early sleep, I was awakened around midnight by a tremendous clanging. I recognized the noise as being related to institutional steam heat, but I had never heard pipes so loud or so resonant; the whole room vibrated. When the noise didn't subside I got up to look for the perpetrating radiator, but it was embedded in a paneled Tudor wall behind a brass Tudor grill. I tugged at the grillwork, hoping to reach in and turn off a valve. But it had been seamlessly welded. The radiator was beyond human reach—and had been since the age of Gatsby.

Back in bed, I tried to smother the noise, but it pierced all the pillows I put over my head, and around 1:30 I pulled on my pants and went down the winding staircase to the front hall, where a night clerk was on duty. "Please come with me," I said, leading him back up. Before we even reached the top of the stairs we heard a metallic rat-tat-tat. The clerk was amazed. "Where's it coming from?" he asked. I told him it was coming from Mr. Wilson's bedroom. "I've never heard anything like *that* before," he said. He followed me to the radiator, studied its Tudor defenses and said there was nothing he could do. I told him he had to find me another bed, and we poked down the sleeping corridors until we came to a small cell that I took to be a former chambermaid's room, and there at last I found repose.

I slept until 9, having no early obligations, and padded back down the hall to Mr. Wilson's bedroom, where I had left my disheveled bed and belongings. I shaved and took a shower in Mr. Wilson's immense marble bathroom and emerged, wearing only a towel, to find myself being observed by three women in Mrs. Wilson's bedroom, on the far side of the velvet rope. I realized that Meadow Brook Hall, having fed its overnight guests and sent them off to their writers' workshops, had shifted into tourist mode and was now showing the Wilson house to sightseers. One sight it hadn't expected to show them was me.

Dressing warily, I went downstairs to eat. But Meadow Brook Hall was now moving to its own Saturday rhythm. Breakfast was over, and the last thing anyone wanted to see was a leftover visiting lecturer. Nobody knew where I was supposed to give my talk or how I was supposed to get there; it was one of those modern campuses with look-alike buildings with sound-alike names. When someone from the writing conference finally remembered to come and get me I was pitifully grateful, and as I bade farewell to Meadow Brook Hall I heard something click that wasn't Mr. Wilson's radiator. It was my Holiday Inn policy being born.

Today I never visit a college without stopping at the airport newsstand to load up on Hershey bars and Planter's peanuts, and those two quick-energy foods have often been my savior. What I've learned is not to be fooled by the efficiency of the original phone call inviting me to give a talk. Once the speaker is safely hooked, little thought goes into what he will need when he eventually shows up.

I've become an expert on lecterns: the ones that nobody remembered to provide ("I think I saw one in a closet down on the first floor"); the ones that are in the wrong position; the ones that are waist-high; the ones that have no light; the ones that have a light whose bulb is out. I was once introduced in a darkened auditorium by a professor who made a point of telling the audience how eagerly the college had been looking forward to my visit. In fact he had had four months to get ready. But the lectern, when I joined him there, was as dark as the auditorium. "Does this light work?" I asked him. "I'm sure it does," he said, flicking the switch. It didn't work. He shrugged and took his seat. I smiled—the long-practiced "Oh, it's nothing, really" smile—and tried to ad-lib the talk I had carefully written.

A scenario that befalls me remarkably often goes like this. I've been invited to give a talk at a college that has close ties with its town. The talk has been advertised for 7:30 in Frothingham Hall, and it's open to the public. When I arrive I'm told that "some English department people" would like to have an early dinner with me. "This town doesn't have any good restaurants," my host says, "but there's a steak house called the Twin Poplars ten miles out on I-29, and we're all going to meet there at 5:45." The drive to the Twin Poplars feels more than ten miles long, but we find it, and the other men and women straggle in. I don't flatter myself that they have come to hear my insights. They have come because they don't often get to eat out.

Drinks are served, and then dinner, and at seven we are just ordering dessert. My stomach is not at rest. Unlike my host,

I've been looking at my watch, and I mention that we should probably be on our way. He gets the check and signs for it—another ten minutes—and we leave the other professors and sprint to his car. Out on I-29, my host realizes that he doesn't know how to get back to town. "That sign said North," he says. "Do you think I should have turned left back there?" It's *his* town; I'm from New York. "My wife's the one who usually makes this drive," he explains. "Keep your eye out for an overpass somewhere along here."

At 7:25 we careen into the parking lot of Frothingham Hall, which surprises my host by being full. It's full of the cars of people who have come to hear my talk. "You go on in while I find a place to park," he says, shoving me out. "Professor Smithers is going to introduce you. You'll recognize him—he's got a beard." Rushing through the door, I'm hustled down the aisle and launched onto the stage like a projectile. It's exactly 7:30. Afterward a professor offers to drive me to the airport the next day. I'm not surprised when he goes two exits past the airport; many of my hosts have been unable to find their own airport.

None of this has anything to do with bad intentions. Everyone who has invited me to a college has wanted nothing but the best for me, and I value the friendships I made on those visits. I'm talking about the gap between intention and execution. After falling into that chasm again and again I began to think about damage control. I now make it my business to supervise all kinds of details that shouldn't have to be my business. I telephone the college in advance to discuss the lectern. When I'm dropped off at my motel I ask who I should call if the person who is supposed to pick me up doesn't pick me up. I opt to eat at the college cafeteria and not at the Twin Poplars. I insist on getting to the hall in time to check out the lectern and the sound system. I remind my hosts what time it is. On the highway I point out the sign that says Airport.

Such hard-won lessons, I once thought, were mine alone. But then I began to meet other voyagers on the college trail, and as we talked we found that our experiences were almost identical. "That's just what happened to me," they say after every recollection of a missed turn on the road back to town or a missed night's sleep in a college guest house. But I can make one claim that's unique. Nobody else got put up in Mr. Wilson's bedroom.

Those trips around America to teach writing—at colleges, schools, newspapers, businesses and government agencies—became a regular part of my life after my book *On Writing Well* was published in 1976. The book grew out of a course I was then teaching at Yale.

I became a teacher by deliberately uprooting my life. I had already uprooted it once by leaving the *Herald Tribune*. When I was hired in 1946 it was the best-written and best-edited newspaper in the country—a constellation of journalists at the top of their form. The older editors who made us rewrite what we had written—and rewritten—weren't doing it just for our own good; it was for the honorableness of the craft. They were custodians of the best. Theirs were the values I learned as a young reporter, which I've tried to apply to my writing and editing and teaching ever since. I fully expected to stay at the *Herald Tribune* for the rest of my working life.

But soon after World War II the paper began to lose money. Newsprint and labor costs soared, and the *Trib* could no longer compete with the affluent *New York Times* for the same upscale readers and advertisers. The owners' response was to cheapen the paper with gimmicks they hoped would attract the masses: tawdry gossip columns, a green sports section, an "early bird" edition that went on sale at 8 P.M. In small increments they eroded the character of their paper and drove away many of its best reporters and editors and readers. The masses also stayed away; they knew when they were being patronized.

I gradually began to see that the *Herald Tribune*'s standards were now lower than *my* standards. I don't want to work for people I don't respect, and one day in 1959 I walked into George Cornish's office one last time and said I was quitting. When I called Caroline to tell her, she said, "What are you going to do now?" I thought it was a fair question—by then we had a one-year-old daughter. I said, "I guess I'm a freelance writer."

And that's what I was for the next 11 years. In the early 1960s it was still possible to be a generalist in America; general magazines hadn't yet lost their big advertisers to television. At first I wrote mainly for the *Saturday Evening Post*. Then the *Post* died. Then I wrote a column for *Look*, and *Look* died. (Meanwhile the *Herald Tribune* had also died.) Then I got a contract to write for *Life*, and in five years *Life* would die. My past is littered with the bleached bones of failed journalistic enterprises. All that mortality taught me an important lesson: writers and editors should live in the expectation that they will wake up some morning and find that their bosses have left during the night. If this happens to you, get on with your life. Don't waste energy railing at the publishing profession. It has been careless with writers forever and isn't going to change.

Freelance writing was not only risky; it also was a lonely life. Even Amy and John got to leave home and go off to nursery school and kindergarten. Caroline enrolled in graduate school and got started on a long and valuable career as an educator and a scholar of child development. The apartment was too quiet. I'm not a writer who yearns for a cottage in the woods; I wouldn't get to the first semicolon in that cottage. I need the roar of buses and taxis—evidence of life support just outside the door.

One day in 1968 Caroline said, "I wonder what it would be like for us to live somewhere besides New York." It was a heretical notion to put to a fourth-generation New Yorker. But I began to discuss the idea with friends, and one of them, Eric Larrabee, an editor who had uprooted his own life, said, "You know, change is a tonic." I *didn't* know that; I was afraid of change. But I seized on the phrase, and it gave me the energy to proceed. I had always wanted to teach—to give back some of the things I had learned. But where? We wouldn't want to live in the suburbs or out in the country. What else was a possibility? Maybe a college town. Maybe we could make a satisfying life in an academic community.

I decided to give it a shot. I went to my typewriter and

started writing letters to college presidents and provosts and deans all across America. I told them I wanted to teach a course in nonfiction writing. I explained that I wouldn't cost the college much because I would be mainly supported by my contract with *Life*. I didn't think any first-rate college would have me; I was a journalist, God forbid, with only a B.A. degree. I therefore focused on colleges that had an innovative bent. One that responded warmly was the University of California's lively new campus at Santa Cruz, and Caroline and I flew out there to look it over. We also went to Sarasota for an interview at New College, a progressive newcomer in the University of Florida system. But neither place seemed right for our family.

Meanwhile I kept hearing back from all the presidents and provosts and deans. Their letters were generous; nobody told me I was crazy. But as administrators they were enmeshed in the machinery of academic delay: three-year plans, five-year plans, steering committees, curriculum reviews. This was a door that wouldn't be opened quickly, if at all.

Still, I kept at it. I've never spent any time moping about rejection. When one of my articles comes back with a note saying "I'm afraid it isn't quite right for us," or "It doesn't quite suit our needs at the moment," I don't shake my fist at the editor for not recognizing the jewel he was offered. I type a new covering letter and get my article back in the mailbox by noon. Again: don't weaken yourself with negative energy. If you're a writer you'll need all the positive energy you can generate.

Now, as the rejections piled up, I broadened my campaign.

I wrote to all kinds of people who had some kind of college connection. Many were friends and acquaintances; some were people I had never met but whose work I admired. Maybe one of them would hear of something. The overture from Santa Cruz had been arranged by the sociologist David Riesman, whose book *The Lonely Crowd* was then a bestseller. He didn't know me, but someone sent him my letter, and he wrote to Santa Cruz on my behalf. Such generosity! I believe that one thing leads to another. If you tell enough people about your hopes and dreams, someday a circle will connect.

My circle finally connected—almost two years after I started writing all those letters. One night in the winter of 1970 I got a call from R. W. B. Lewis, master of Calhoun College at Yale and a distinguished professor of English and American literature. Someone had sent him my letter. Lewis said he knew my work, and he invited me to teach my course at his college on an experimental basis for one term. On that slender thread Caroline and I sold our apartment and moved to New Haven, a city where we had never set foot, to try our luck at living somewhere besides New York.

I gave my course a plain title, "Nonfiction Workshop," and it was listed in the Yale College catalogue. At registration time more than 170 students signed up. That's 150 more than a writing teacher can teach well, and most of the applicants had to be turned away. What caused the huge sign-up, I think, was a change in the cultural weather. We had moved to Yale in the fall of 1970—the first term following the tumultuous spring of protests against the Vietnam War that shook colleges all across the country and shut some of them down. Yale had famously survived a severe threat of violence connected to a Black Panther trial in New Haven.

When that endless spring finally ended, the nation was exhausted and the counterculture was dead. At Yale, when we arrived, all was calm; it was as if the '60s never happened. The students had only one agenda—to get an education—and one of the things they wanted to learn was how to write clearly. During the permissive '60s their high school English teachers had urged them to "let it all hang out," regardless of grammar or syntax. Now they found they had been deprived of knowing how to express themselves: how to harness the world they lived in. My course looked like salvation in the desert.

The students' cry for help wasn't lost on Yale's English Department. At that time the department was the epicenter of "deconstruction" and other faddish studies in the clinical analysis of texts. Its emphasis was not on how to write but on how to dissect what other people had written. The great writers on the Yale faculty weren't the English professors; they were the history professors—robust stylists like Edmund S. Morgan, C. Vann Woodward, George Pierson, Jonathan Spence and John Morton Blum. Now the English Department rallied to the rescue of the plain declarative sentence. As a stopgap it hired several other journalists from New York to teach courses that roughly replicated mine. Then it went about building its own strong program of expository writing—a commitment that is still in place.

Meanwhile I continued to teach my own course, as well as

a course in humor writing. In choosing my students I always tried for a broad mixture. I didn't just want aspiring journalists; I was also looking for the next Rachel Carson or Oliver Sacks—scientists who could make their complex worlds accessible to the rest of us. Or the next David McCullough or Edmund Morris—biographers who can reconstruct an era and a life. As it turned out, many of my students did become writers and editors—for the *New York Times*, *The New Yorker*, the *Atlantic Monthly* and other publications. But my goal was to teach young men and women in every discipline to write clearly and warmly and well.

Two events propelled me into the larger life of the Yale community. In the fall of 1970 the *Yale Alumni Magazine* unexpectedly lost both its editor and its managing editor. The board, hearing that a real live journalist had come to town, asked me if I would like to be the editor. At first it seemed like an absurd thing for a middle-aged Princeton man to do. But my second thought was: what quicker way to learn about the great university that had taken me in? The magazine had a readership that any editor would covet—it was sent to all 110,000 alumni of Yale College and of the university's ten graduate schools; almost no field of learning was outside its domain. Editors are licensed to be curious, and for seven years I edited the magazine and pampered my curiosity. (Note to writers and editors: if it sounds interesting, do it.)

Then, in 1973, I was appointed by President Kingman Brewster to be master of Branford College, one of Yale's 12 undergraduate residential colleges. Every college has a resident master who presides over its life as an academic and social community. Branford was the college that was on all the postcards and all the guided tours: a handsome Gothic quadrangle at the very center of the campus. Our family moved into the master's house and stayed for six years, all four of us caught up in the domestic rhythms of the 400 young men and women who lived in our midst, never surprised by a knock on the door at some odd hour. (Caroline also had her own work, as head of a local school.) The iconic Harkness Tower and its carillon loomed overhead, and we soon learned that a little bit of carillon can go a long way.

Being a college master was the perfect cure for the loneliness of the freelance writer; like any pastoral job, it consisted of small personal encounters from morning to night. But the only writing I ever did about those years was a long magazine article called "College Pressures," which described four kinds of pressure that I felt were turning Yale undergraduates into workaholics obsessed with high grades. One was parental pressure to succeed, often in subjects that would prepare them for careers in medicine or law that they really didn't want to enter. Another was financial pressure: the need to pay back all those student loans. The third was peer pressure—the belief that their fellow students were getting higher grades—and the fourth, worst of all, was self-imposed pressure.

> I tell my students [the article continued] there is no one "right" way to get ahead—that each of them is a different person, starting from a different point and bound for a different destination. I tell them that change is a tonic and that all the slots are not codified or the frontiers

closed. One of my ways of telling them is to hold a master's tea every Wednesday afternoon. I invite men and women who have achieved success outside the academic world—people that Yale students might otherwise never meet—to come and talk informally about their work. They are heads of businesses and ad agencies, editors of magazines, politicians, public officials, television producers, Broadway producers, filmmakers, artists, writers, musicians, photographers, scientists, historians—a mixed bag of achievers.

I ask them first to say a few words about how they got their start. The students assume that they started in their present field and knew all along that it was what they wanted to do. Luckily for me, most of them got into their field by a circuitous route, to their surprise, after many detours. The students are startled. They can hardly conceive of a career that was not preplanned. They can hardly imagine allowing the hand of God or chance to nudge them down some unforeseen trail.

That article, first published in 1979, has been constantly reprinted in textbooks and anthologies ever since. I'm sorry about that; it's one form of income I'd gladly give up. I don't want that article to be as pertinent today as it was 25 years ago. In fact, it's more pertinent. What I want for all young people is a release from the clammy grip of the future. I'd like them to savor each step of their education as a rich experience in itself, not as a preparation for the next step.

The friendships I made with all those Branford students and

faculty fellows have nourished me ever since. I still run into my students everywhere, especially on the sidewalks of New York. Behind the accretions of paunch and gray hair I can still glimpse the boy or girl who threw a Frisbee in Branford court or sat across the table in the dining hall. The two richest friendships have been with the French-horn player Willie Ruff and the pianist Dwike Mitchell, of the Mitchell-Ruff jazz duo. Ruff, who lived in the college, was a professor at the Yale School of Music. He had recently persuaded Yale to hold a convocation honoring 40 of America's greatest black musicians and dancers—Duke Ellington, Dizzy Gillespie, Benny Carter, Odetta, Marian Anderson, Charlie Mingus, Paul Robeson, Honi Coles—and naming them Duke Ellington Fellows. Ruff's idea was that those men and women would periodically come back to perform for students at Yale and in New Haven's predominantly black public schools. Every year Ruff shepherded those giants through our lives, starting with a concert in the Branford College dining hall. Dwike Mitchell, who lived in New York, was always there to accompany them. He was the best jazz pianist I ever heard.

After I moved back to New York I began to take lessons from Mitchell and to follow the two men around as a writer. In 1981 I went with them to Shanghai, where they introduced live jazz to China, and in 1983 I went with Ruff to Venice, where he played Gregorian chants on the French horn in St. Mark's cathedral at night to study the acoustics that inspired the Venetian school of music. Both of those articles ran in *The New Yorker* and later became part of my dual biography, *Willie and Dwike*. Republished in 2000 as *Mitchell & Ruff*, it has found a new life as a teaching book in schools, and I still follow my two friends around, joining them in workshops where we try to tease out the connections between writing and music.

The fact that Yale let me do all these things is my reason for telling the story. By tradition Yale's college masters were established professors on the faculty. I was a layman from out of nowhere. But the university gave me its trust and gave me an academic life; I was never patronized for not being an academic myself. For that large-hearted gift I've always been grateful, and I commend my story to everyone who has arrived at a moment of choice: seniors graduating from college, adults stuck in a dead-end job and yearning for a change of direction. Your options are not as limited as you think. Don't assume that the people you would like to work for have defined their needs as narrowly as you suppose. Sell yourself as something new and different.

Extending that advice to writers, I would say: Don't assume that editors know exactly what they want. Often they don't. Don't shape yourself to a dumb assignment; that's no favor to you or to the magazine or to the reader. Shape the assignment to your own strengths and curiosities. Or come up with a better idea. You make your own luck. One thing leads to another. Change is a tonic. This book is sprinkled with maxims that are clichés of positive thinking. But they have worked for me, and you can make them work for you. Give yourself permission to risk the unknown. Dare to not do what the world expects you to do.

The longest-bearing fruit of my decade at Yale is *On Writing Well*. In 1976 I decided to see if I could put my nonfiction writing course into a book. At that time the dominant writing manual was *The Elements of Style*, by William Strunk, Jr., and E. B. White. The book is admired by all serious writers, and I had no wish to jump into the same ring. Instead of competing with Strunk and White's book I would try to complement it. *The Elements of Style* was essentially a book of pointers and admonitions: do this, don't do that. What it *didn't* address was how to apply those principles to all the forms that nonfiction writing can take. That's what I taught in my course, and it's what I would teach in my book: how to write about people and places, science and technology, history and sports, music and art and every other field a nonfiction writer might want to pursue.

The first edition of *On Writing Well* was a slender volume. I had never attempted a how-to book before, and I found myself writing in a new style: my teacher's voice, not my writer's voice, addressing the reader directly ("You'll find . . ."). I didn't say much about my own writing methods, not wanting to intrude myself on the teaching process. But occasionally I allowed myself to break that code of reticence. If I remembered a writing assignment that helped me to solve a problem, I described what I had learned. "If it helped me so much," I would tell myself, justifying the breach of modesty, "it will probably help other writers." That turned out to be an important breakthrough. After the book came out and I began to hear from readers and teachers, I saw that what they were responding to was my willingness to share my own struggles and decisions.

So began a relationship of trust that has deepened ever

since. In the expanded second edition I addressed the questions those early readers raised and wrote new chapters on subjects they thought I should have covered. One new chapter was called "Writing in Your Job." Since then I've revised the book four more times in response to new technologies (the word processor), new social trends (more women writing nonfiction), new demographic trends (more writers from other cultural traditions), new literary trends (more interest in memoir, business, science and sports), and various changes in the language. I also incorporated lessons I learned by writing my books *Spring Training* and *American Places*—two kinds of writing I hadn't tried before—and I wrote a highly personal final chapter on my credo as a writer and the influence and values of my parents.

By now I completely trusted my readers to trust my judgment on what I thought would be helpful to them, however personal or quirky the anecdote I might dredge up to illustrate a point. In 1993 I began teaching an adult course called "People and Places" at the New School, in New York, which reflects my growing interest in the intangibles that produce good writing, and this has led to new chapters on such values as enjoyment and intention. In every new edition the new material consisted of lessons I learned since the previous edition by setting myself new writing tasks. Meanwhile I kept thinning out what was no longer pertinent or useful.

Today *On Writing Well* has sold well over a million copies, continuing to complement *The Elements of Style*. If its longevity contains any advice for writers of self-help books, the main lesson is that I make myself available. Readers don't feel that they're hearing from a professor of rhetoric; they're hearing from another working writer. My initial fear of immodesty, I see, was misguided. The best teachers of an art or a craft are their own best textbook. Students who take courses from those teachers—writers, painters, musicians, dancers, gardeners, cooks—really want to know how their teachers do what they do. They may not like the teacher's work and may eventually reject it. But at least they have a model to think about and to emulate, or to rebel against or outgrow. Therefore have confidence in your accumulated knowledge and make yourself available.

The other lesson is a matter of style. Writers are always impatient to find their style, as if they expect it to descend on them, heaven-sent, in their twenties or early thirties. Usually it takes longer; we grow into our style. I could argue that I didn't really find my style until I wrote *On Writing Well*, in my fifties. Until then my style more probably reflected who I wanted to be perceived as—the urbane essayist or columnist or humorist—than who I really was. Only when I began to write as a teacher and had no agenda except to be helpful—to pass along what I knew—did my style become integrated with my personality and my character. Now, whatever I write about, I make myself available. No hiding.

In 1979 a number of signs and portents told me it was time to get back to my home town and to my primary work as a writer and editor. Physically, I was worn out from trying to piece together so many jobs; in 1977 I had also written a weekly column for the newly created Home section of the *New York Times*. I was also contending with a rash of separations: my father died, my retina detached, Amy was away at college, and Caroline returned to New York to become director of the Bank Street School for Children. Only John and I were left in the big house, and he would be off to college in the fall. Above all, I needed a steady income. Unlike Yale's other college masters, who had their professor's salaries and benefits, I had no tenure and no security for the future; I was a freelance master and I was a freelance teacher, loosely attached to the Yale English Department. Altogether I had been freelancing for 20 years. My life badly needed stabilizing.

But what kind of job could I get? By now I was well beyond an age that employers find endearing. Would the old maxims work for me one more time? Did one thing still lead to another? I wasn't so sure. It was a low moment, and I didn't like the feeling.

There was only one thing to do. I went back to my typewriter—the same aging Underwood on which I had written all those letters to college presidents and provosts and deans—and made a résumé. The Branford seniors, job-seekers themselves, showed me how to do it—how to make it look nice—and I sent it with an accompanying letter to a cross section of people I had known in my former life in New York.

Again, the days passed and the phone didn't ring. But then, one day, it did. Two people who received my résumé happened to send it to Al Silverman, president of the Book-of-the-Month Club, who happened to be looking for a senior editor. Could I come to New York for an interview? I could, and did, and met my next lucky angel.

In June, when the academic year ended, I cleaned the family belongings out of the Branford master's house and moved back to New York. There Al Silverman gave me a big office overlooking Lexington Avenue and showed me that there was life after Yale.

9.

Books of the Month

TWO FACTS—FURTHER PROOF that one thing leads to another—may have helped to persuade Al Silverman that I was the editor he was looking for. One was that *On Writing Well* was a popular alternate selection of the Book-of-the-Month Club. The other was that I wouldn't be coming to the club as a stranger. In 1966 I had been hired by its founder, Harry Scherman, to write a history of the club on the occasion of its 40th anniversary and its 200-millionth book. Scherman knew my work because I had written a brochure several years earlier to accompany a special recording of Bach's B Minor Mass that the club had prepared for its members.

The invitation to write a history of Scherman's company appealed to me. The Book-of-the-Month Club wasn't just a business; it was an institution—one of those lucky firms that have slipped into the American vocabulary, instantly recognized in jokes and conversations. I remembered a cartoon in the *New Yorker* by Helen Hokinson that showed one of her earnest ladies breaking the difficult news to her local librarian: "I'm afraid this is good-bye, Miss MacDonald. I'm joining the Book-of-the-Month Club." I remembered how the club seemed to have furnished the bookshelves of half the families I knew when I was growing up; its distinctive titles— Winston Churchill's stately histories of World War II, Will and Ariel Durant's *The Story of Civilization*—were fixtures of the national decor. I remembered that I once received a gift membership in the club and was sent a succession of carefully chosen books—atlases and anthologies and other useful volumes—that I wouldn't have bought on my own. Somebody at the club was taking me seriously. But who?

I found the Book-of-the-Month Club at 345 Hudson Street, a drab thoroughfare of factories and warehouses in lower Manhattan. It wasn't an address that said "literature." Harry Scherman was a small, courtly man of 79 who looked exactly like what he was: a self-made entrepreneur in the twilight of a satisfying life. He had hatched one of the brilliant marketing ideas of the 20th century—the book club—and had started a company to put his idea to work. Like every patriarch who has founded a family business, he was surrounded by family—or at least by people he regarded as family. In the front offices, editors sat reading manuscripts. In a huge back room, women sat at desks with card files and Addressograph machines, processing the daily flow of orders. It was one man's company, kindly and paternalistic. The help got paid in cash.

But at the center of it all was a bone-deep love of books. When Harry Scherman talked to me about his company he was young again, still marveling at the power of books to excite him, still eager to be surprised by a writer with something new to say and a fresh voice to say it in. As he reminisced about the club's first 40 years I saw that the books themselves had become characters in his life, pushing their way to attention by the force of their personality. In his passion for quality he reminded me of my father talking about shellac.

Now it was 13 years later and the company had moved uptown to 485 Lexington Avenue, far from the industrial clatter of Hudson Street. In certain obvious ways much had changed. Scherman had died in 1969 and was succeeded by his son-in-law Axel Rosin, who broadened the business by forming a half-dozen smaller clubs such as the Quality Paperback Club. The women with the card files and Addressograph machines were gone; a modern plant and warehouse had been built in Camp Hill, Pennsylvania, to handle the members' accounts and to ship their books. Above all, it was no longer a family business. Rosin, approaching retirement himself, had gone looking for a buyer and had sold the company to Time, Inc.

But on a deeper level nothing was different. The place where I went to work in the summer of 1979 still had the quiet air of a college English department, the editors reading in easy chairs, encircled by piles of manuscripts awaiting their judgment. One of those editors told me that a janitor—a man who came around every afternoon to empty the wastebaskets— had recently said to him, "I can't figure out what this company makes. The only thing you people do all day is read." But what mainly reassured me was Al Silverman himself; he struck me as Harry Scherman's natural heir. He believed in the power of books to change people's lives and in the obligation of the club to find the best new books for its members. I assumed that these values had been transmitted by Scherman himself, but the two men never met; Silverman didn't arrive until 1972, having previously been editor of *Sport* magazine. I did, however, find one connection.

"I'm exactly as old as the Book-of-the-Month Club," Silverman told me. "When I was growing up in Lynn, Massachusetts, my aunt Rose lived with us. She was a high school teacher who taught typing and other skills that young people would need to make it through the Depression. My parents could never afford to buy books. Aunt Rose liked to read books, so she joined the Book-of-the-Month Club. The first book I can remember her receiving was *The Forty Days of Musa Dagh*, by Franz Werfel. My aunt Rose loved it, and the books just kept coming in until she got married and left us.

"I never did read *The Forty Days of Musa Dagh*; I was mostly into *The Book of Knowledge*. In fact, I was a floundering student, and one day my third-grade teacher, Miss Moriarty, called my mother in to see what could be done about me. The best my mother could say was that I liked to look at books. So Miss Moriarty suggested, as a last-ditch possibility, that my mother take me to the library to get me in the habit of reading, and it became a weekly ritual for us to walk to the Parrot Street branch of the Lynn Public Library to drop off the old books and get a new batch. I'll never know whether it was those weekly treks or those books coming into the house from the Book-of-the-Month Club that made a reader of me. I like to think it was the Book-of-the-Month Club, because that's where I ended up earning my living."

That's also where I earned my living for the next eight years. I learned for the first time what it's like to belong to a corporate family. Only the hours—8:30 to 4:30—were a shock to the system. Otherwise the job was a lifesaver. At Yale I had lived with turnover: students constantly moving in and out of my life. Now I was part of a community of men and women united by a fierce love of what they were doing. At that time more than 5,000 books were submitted to the club every year. They came from every nook of the publishing industry: from big publishers in New York and small publishers in Alabama, from foreign publishers and technical publishers and university presses. They arrived cold, seven or eight months before publication, vast mountains of paper, naked of all the blandishments with which they would ultimately woo the customer: the glamorous photograph of the author, the effusive jacket copy, the blurbs from other writers praising the author's insight into the human condition.

Wherever they came from and whatever they looked like, they got a careful reading, and I always looked forward to the Thursday morning meeting at which the in-house editors reported on the week's catch. We met in a conference room that felt like a library, its shelves lined with the books that the club had been sending out since 1926, its walls hung with oil portraits of Harry Scherman and some of the club's original judges—like Dorothy Canfield Fisher, Christopher Morley and William Allen White—who gazed sternly down on our deliberations. The judges were literary eminences who met separately 15 times a year to choose the Main Selection. The rest of us chose the many Alternates that were also offered to the members every month.

The principle by which books got selected was one that those early judges had only slowly stumbled on, as I knew from writing my history. "It took us a long while to learn a very simple truth," Henry Seidel Canby, dean of the first board of judges, explained. "We couldn't choose a book on the basis of what we thought the public wanted. We didn't know. The publishers themselves didn't know. Sometimes in the early years, in a lean month, we would take a just-pretty-good book because we all agreed that this was what the general reader, if not our superior selves, wanted. Those choices often failed and never really succeeded. We realized that there was only one safe procedure, and that was to choose what we ourselves liked. If we liked a book well enough, the public, whose taste was perhaps less discriminating but at least as sound and healthy as ours, seemed to like it, too. But they also wanted leadership. If we gave them a skillful article from the production line they were vaguely disappointed, for they wanted to read books that they liked, but better books, and different books from what they had been reading."

So began the steady march into American homes of good authors who had never been there before. Until then Americans had little access to good literature; they were mainly reading junk like *Ben-Hur*. To look back today over the names of the writers the Book-of-the-Month Club began sending out in the late 1920s—Edith Wharton, Sinclair Lewis, Ellen Glasgow, Elinor Wylie, Carl Sandburg, Stephen Vincent Benet, Pearl S. Buck, Willa Cather, Thornton Wilder, George Santayana, Robert Frost, John Steinbeck—is to see how the club shaped and elevated America's reading habits. Even more striking is the number of foreign authors who were sent forth into a country that was still intellectually provincial. Some of them were English and thus only moderately strange: John Galsworthy, Virginia Woolf, H. G. Wells, A. E. Housman, T. E. Lawrence. But many were total strangers from Europe: Sigrid Undset and Thomas Mann, Antoine de Saint-Exupéry, Andre Malraux and Stefan Zweig, bearing philosophical packages from older cultures that were by no means easy to unwrap.

The case of Isak Dinesen is typical of how the members were pushed into new territory. Dinesen's *Seven Gothic Tales* came to the attention of Dorothy Canfield Fisher in manuscript form in 1934. "The stories were so strange," she said. "I thought they were very fine, highly colored like a new kind of fruit or wine. I had never seen anything like them. I tried them out on several publishers, who promptly returned them and said, 'We can't make anything out of them. What do they mean?' Finally Robert Haas at Random House, who was as puzzled as everyone else, tried them on his colleagues, and they were all crazy about them, even the salesmen. They felt that their strangeness was something precious." So it was by this circuitous route that the Danish author was first published in the United States and introduced to Book-of-the-Month Club members, who loved not only her Gothic tales but her second book, *Out of Africa*, four years later.

Originally the five judges' method had been to take a vote on the books they were considering. But they soon gave it up; the winner tended to be everybody's second choice. Instead they adopted the Quaker system of concurrence (three of them happened to be from Quaker families), whereby, as Canby explained, "if the majority couldn't persuade the minority to concur, the book was dropped, and its subsequent history showed that we were right to do so. Frequently our discussion proved that a book had more vitality than we suspected."

That turned out to be the key to the club's success. "The books themselves impose the final decision," Scherman told me. Which often meant that the judges found themselves out on a limb, having chosen an unorthodox book long before anyone else knew about it. Nobody had heard of J. D. Salinger's *The Catcher in the Rye* when the judges selected it in 1951. Scherman was particularly worried about the title, and at a lunch for Salinger he asked the author if he would change it to something less bizarre. Salinger pondered the request for a moment. Then he said, "Holden Caulfield wouldn't like that."

When I went to work at the Book-of-the-Month Club in 1979 all those beliefs in the primacy of the book were still being jealously guarded, and the affection I had felt for Harry Scherman's company when I first wrote about it came back to me. I was the club's in-house editor, in charge of the *Book-of-*

the-Month Club News and various other club publications. Any task related to teaching and public service also fell in my lap. Al Silverman believed that the club should have an educational presence, and I was the willing executor of his many public-spirited projects.

The one I most enjoyed organizing was an exhibit held at the New York Public Library in 1986 to celebrate the club's 60th anniversary. By then the number of books distributed had reached 440 million, and I wanted to tell the chronological story of how the club created a nation of readers. But I also wanted our exhibit to be a reminder that books don't exist in isolation. They are social organisms, products of their historical moment and propellants of social change. Sixty small display cases were installed in the foyer of the library—one for each year. Each case contained the most important books of the year in their original jackets. At first those books were mainly novels. But gradually, over the decades, the authors also began to include nonfiction writers whose books made a difference in how Americans thought about themselves and about the world: Rachel Carson, Ralph Nader, Benjamin Spock, Norman Vincent Peale, Betty Friedan. To accompany the books I found artifacts of events that gave the year a larger cultural significance: theater playbills, movie stills, newspaper headlines, *Life* magazine covers, programs of concerts and ballets and art exhibitions, photographs of pioneering feats in science and technology and architecture and design.

Here are a few examples of what the display cases contained, as described in the brief panels I wrote for each case:

[1928]

A popular epic poem about the Civil War, *John Brown's Body*, proved that readers weren't afraid of a story told in verse, and *Coming of Age in Samoa* made household words of anthropology and Margaret Mead. But the event that would most affect the American landscape took place in Germany. The Bauhaus School closed and its many innovative architects and designers (Walter Gropius, Mies van der Rohe) flocked to this country. One of them, Marcel Breuer, introduced in 1928 what was to become America's most popular chair.

[1930]

Sinclair Lewis wrote *Babbitt* and became the first American to win the Nobel Prize. From Paris came an elephant named Babar who would be one of the all-time charmers of children. The Museum of Modern Art established a department of photography, certifying as an art what most people thought was only a hobby, and the graceful Chrysler Building set a standard of architecture and design by which all future skyscrapers would be measured.

[1932]

More Hemingway (Ernest discovers bullfighting), plus two books as durable as they were different: Dashiell Hammett's thin man would never live in Laura Ingalls Wilder's little house in the big woods. It was a year of fabulous launches: two classics of radio humor (Fred

Allen and Jack Benny), one classic entertainment palace (Radio City Music Hall), one classic ape (King Kong), and the Folger Shakespeare Library. But the hit song was "Brother, Can You Spare a Dime?"

[1935]

Clarence Day's *Life with Father* introduced a character so enduring that when his book was later made into a play it ran almost forever. But the year was George Gershwin's: his dynamic opera *Porgy and Bess* would become America's most exhilarating cultural export. *Top Hat* established Fred Astaire and Ginger Rogers as the definition of elegance in dance, and Monopoly began what would be an even longer run than *Life with Father.*

[1946]

Two books would alter America's thinking. John Hersey's *Hiroshima* brought the atomic bomb into our hearts and minds. Dr. Spock's *Baby and Child Care* reared the first generation that had to live with the bomb—and that would reshape a whole set of national attitudes when, in the 1960s, it grew up.

[1952]

Positive thinking was in: Norman Vincent Peale made it a creed and E. B. White's Charlotte, spinning her web, made it a pleasure. Ralph Ellison defined the black experience in two words: *Invisible Man.* Gary Cooper shot the baddies at high noon: America's favorite morality

tale at the top of its form. Jazz went to college with
Dave Brubeck and hooked a whole new audience.

[1957]

Kerouac, Pasternak and Dr. Seuss: an unlikely trio of
authors came and saw and conquered. *West Side Story*
was the quintessential fusion of the arts—Leonard
Bernstein's music, Stephen Sondheim's lyrics, Jerome
Robbins' dances and Shakespeare's *Romeo and Juliet*.
And what's that new sound coming out of Detroit?

One artifact that I knew I wanted, for the year 1934, was
the program for the premiere of *Four Saints in Three Acts*, the
opera by Gertrude Stein and Virgil Thomson, performed at
the Wadsworth Atheneum in Hartford, one of the brilliant
cultural events of the decade. I had kept in touch with
Thomson over the years, and I called him at the apartment
where he famously lived in the Chelsea Hotel, a New York
landmark adorned with plaques commemorating the many
artistic and literary giants who stayed there, including Mark
Twain, Thomas Wolfe and Dylan Thomas. A recent PBS
documentary about Thomson had shown him in residence
at the Chelsea, composing in bed, the music manuscript
pages arrayed across his Buddha-like stomach. After his own
death he would join the plaqued honorees on the facade of
the hotel.

I asked Thomson if I could come down and borrow the
Wadsworth Atheneum program for my exhibit.

"Of course," he said.

"May I bring my son?" I asked.

"Of course," he said. Thomson was then 88 and John was 26, just getting started on his career as an artist. He was the same age I was when I first met Thomson at the *Herald Tribune* early in my own career.

Thomson met John and me at the door. "You go talk to my assistant," he told me. "I want to talk to this young man." While the assistant and I riffled through the files of *Four Saints in Three Acts* in a side room, Thomson sat with John and talked about the paintings on his walls and about the Paris art scene in the 1920s.

Five years later John and his fiancée, Candace Osborn, also an artist, were apartment-hunting, looking for a first home that wouldn't be just another boring apartment for the newly married. One day they happened to be walking on West 23rd Street and passed the Chelsea. An old memory clicked in: it was possible to be an artist and live satisfyingly in the Chelsea. "I wonder if they have any apartments," John said. They did, and John and Candace lived there contentedly for seven years, leaving only when they were about to become parents. One of John's paintings was hung in the lobby. Such are the continuities of New York life.

By 1987 the Book-of-the-Month Club had run out of interesting things for me to do. It had increasingly become the creature of its corporate owners; sober M.B.A.'s from Time, Inc., buzzed through the halls with 30-day plans and 90-day plans and five-year plans and exhortations to "grow" the company. I don't remember hearing them talk about books. A few years later they would move everybody across town into the Time-Life Building and gradually absorb the club's identity. I resigned in 1987, uprooting my life one more time, to get back to my own writing and editing and teaching. Al Silverman left soon afterward and began a vigorous new career as an editor and writer.

But the company that Harry Scherman founded had a remarkably long run, its values intact for well over six decades. In 1996, when I gave my papers to the Fales Library at New York University, some of my friends asked me why I hadn't given them to Princeton, my alma mater, or to Yale, where I taught. I said I was a New York writer and I had worked for two of New York's great mom-and-pop stores: the *Herald Tribune* and the Book-of-the-Month Club. My papers felt as if they belonged in New York.

What I took away from the Book-of-the-Month Club was a belief that the best books—the most enduring books and the most useful books—are written out of some inner core of conviction. The person who put that idea in my head was Clifton Fadiman. Fadiman had been a cultural icon to me, almost as long as I can remember. He was the urbane host of "Information, Please!" the radio quiz show that our family listened to with slavish regularity when I was growing up. For ten years he was the literary critic of *The New Yorker*, bringing to that role an easy erudition that had no taint of snobbery; he was a man who had read broadly but who respected the best of the popular. He was also a born anthologizer, seemingly under some compulsion to collect for other readers the words and ideas that had enriched his own life.

When I joined the company in 1979, Fadiman was 75 and had been a member of its judges' panel since 1944. For an elder statesman there was nothing "elder" about him. He came east from Santa Barbara every three weeks for the meeting that chose the Main Selection, having read more books than anyone else since the previous judges' session. Somehow he also found time to compile his three-volume *World Treasury of Children's Literature*, having learned enough Swedish, Italian, Spanish and Dutch—in addition to German and French, which he already knew—to "get a feeling for children's books in those languages." When he went blind in his nineties he hired a reader to read the new books to him, calling in his reports to the club almost until he died at 95.

But for Fadiman literature wasn't the ultimate prize. His god was education. "One trend the Book-of-the-Month Club has hooked into from the beginning," he told me, "is the serious American interest in self-education. I'm thinking, for instance, of Lewis Thomas's books, like *Lives of a Cell*, or Barbara Tuchman's histories, or the Durants' *Story of Civilization*. Without the club those books would never have had the impact we gave them by offering them in the first place and by continuing to distribute them over many years—in the case of the Durants, almost fifty years.

"What do our members, in the depths of their being, hanker for? They want books that explain our terrifying age honestly. It can be fiction. John Cheever asks us to look at the frustrations of a large and prosperous middle class, and while he doesn't say, 'This is the way out,' he does throw a real light. In nonfiction, historians like Barbara Tuchman help us to understand our own times. Of course that's been true of writers for hundreds of years, but our age is so scary and fractionated that we need this kind of help more than people did in the 19th century. We thirst for books that put together pieces of the jigsaw puzzle.

"I'll bet if you look at a list of books we've sold most of, you'll find that a majority are books that explain. William L. Shirer explained a whole age to us in *The Rise and Fall of the Third Reich*." (Shirer's book is the club's all-time biggest seller for a single volume.) "And look at all the books that the club sells on health and mental health, or on cooking and gardening and home repair. They're all part of a didactic tradition that goes back at least to Emerson and his interest in self-reliance. Don't forget, this is where pragmatism arose: this is the country of Dewey and James and Peirce. People who came to America had to solve a lot of practical problems—all at once. Very few people came to this country with a million dollars in their pocket."

Good advice for a writer to keep in mind: make your writing useful. I kept Fadiman's words somewhere in my mind when I left the world of the regular paycheck and went back out into the cold.

10.

How to Write a Memoir

THE 1990S WERE THE decade of the memoir. Never had personal narratives gushed so profusely out of the American soil. Everybody had a story to tell, and everybody was telling it. It was the best of times for the form, producing many writers who recalled their early lives with sensitivity and grace, like Frank McCourt, author of *Angela's Ashes*, and Mary Karr, author of *The Liars' Club*.

It was also the worst of times, producing a torrent of memoirs that wallowed in self-pity and self-revelation. Until then memoir writers tended to stop short of full disclosure, cloaking with modesty their most private and shameful memories. Now, suddenly, no episode was too sordid, no family too dysfunctional, to be trotted out for the wonderment of the masses in books and magazines and on talk shows.

The uses and misuses of memoir were much on my mind during the 1990s. In 1993 I began teaching an adult course called "People and Places" at the New School. My students are mainly men and women who want to know how to use writing to try to understand who they are, who they once were, and what heritage they were born into. Their biggest problem, year after year, is how to get control of their story: how to organize its many layers of remembered fact and emotion. My biggest job, year after year, is to help them to select, focus and reduce. Their biggest fear is that they won't be able to do justice to the story they want to tell. My biggest exhortation to them is to believe in the validity of their life and to write about it with confidence and enjoyment. This book is a distillation of that course, just as *On Writing Well* grew out of the undergraduate course I taught at Yale.

Another project that kept me thinking about the form was my book *Inventing the Truth: The Art and Craft of Memoir*. In 1986 Al Silverman created an annual series of lectures, sponsored by the Book-of-the-Month Club and held at the New York Public Library, in which six writers would give talks about a particular genre of writing. The theme of the first series was American biography. As the editor in charge of the series, I told the speakers we didn't want authors lecturing about a genre; we wanted writers talking about how they do what they do, and they responded generously, beginning with David McCullough, who was then in the early research stages of his great biography of Harry Truman.

"You have to know a great deal that you can't get from

books, or even from printed records, such as letters, diaries and contemporary newspaper accounts," McCullough told us. "You have to know the territory. You can't know Harry Truman if you don't know Jackson County, Missouri. Just last weekend I was talking to a man—and this is what happens when you're lucky—who grew up on an adjoining farm, and he told me that the first time he saw Harry Truman was when Harry came in with a wagon at threshing time, and he remembers him distinctly because he was wearing a white Panama hat." Why Harry was wearing a white Panama hat says a lot about the young Truman and about the man he would become—and also about his biographer, modestly attributing this small gem of information to luck. Good writers make their own luck, and I still remember how much I enjoyed hearing that story. We were sitting on a snowy Monday night in the New York Public Library, where so many writers have written so many books, and McCullough was telling us about a man he had tracked down on Saturday in Missouri who had known Truman 70 years earlier. "I talk to people," McCullough said, "who talked to people who came up the Missouri River in the 1840s, when Jackson County was the frontier. It's that close."

We were off to a good start. The lectures in that first series were recorded, and I edited the transcripts into a book called *Extraordinary Lives: The Art and Craft of American Biography*. The following year I chose memoir as our theme, inviting writers whose books had recalled childhoods as different as Jewish Brooklyn (Alfred Kazin), Presbyterian Pittsburgh (Annie Dillard) and Depression-battered New Jersey (Russell

Baker). Again, the talks were recorded, and I edited them into *Inventing the Truth*. Four more books—on religious writing, travel writing, the political novel and writing for children—would follow in the next four years.

One of the stories told in *Inventing the Truth* has been unusually helpful to me as a teacher of memoir, and I'd like to pass it on. Here is Russell Baker describing his first stab at writing the book about the Depression that became *Growing Up*:

Being a good reporter, I had no concept of how to write a memoir. I knew nothing about it; I only knew how to report a magazine piece. So I took my tape recorder out and I interviewed many of my relatives, those who were still living—people in their eighties, one or two in their nineties—about the family, things I had never been interested in before. And my wife Mimi and I began doing the genealogy. Who were these people? I had no notion of who they were or where they had come from. And in the process I began to learn how interesting they were. They were people who would be extremely boring to read about in the newspaper, but they were fascinating. And I transcribed all these interviews and notes. I reported everything very carefully: a long piece of newspaper reportage.

Then I started writing, and what I wrote was a reporter's book in which I quoted these elderly people talking about what life was like long ago in that time and place. I was reporting my own life, and, being the good journalist, I kept myself out of it. And because I was uneasy about what had always been an awkward relationship with my mother and because she wasn't there to testify for herself, I kept *her* out of it. And I wrote a rather long book. I think it ran to four hundred and fifty pages in manuscript.

I was very pleased with it, and I sent it off to my agent and my editor and I thought, "Well, I'll give them twenty-four hours to sit up all night and read it and they'll phone me back tomorrow." Well, there was no phone call the next day, nor the day after. Nobody called the next week, nor the week after that. A month passed and nobody called . . . Eventually I began to sense that there was something wrong, and one night I took it out of the drawer and sat down in my office and started to read. I nodded off on about page 20. And I thought, "If *I* can't read this thing . . ." But it was an intensely responsible book. Everything in it was correct, the quotations were accurate, everything had been double-checked. Finally Tom Congdon, my editor, in despair, asked for a conference . . .

But by that time I had made a second judgment myself that the book was in terrible shape, and I knew what was wrong with it: My mother wasn't in it. There were all these interesting relatives, the uncles and the aunts and people talking from the present about the old days, but it was really nothing but journalism—reminiscences of today about yesterday. I had lunch with Tom and I said that I knew what was wrong with the book and that I would rewrite the whole thing. I said it was a book about a boy and his mother. It was about the tension between a child and his mother, and everything had to hinge on that. And Tom said he thought that was right—that I had made a grievous mistake in trying to write a book about myself in which I didn't appear. He didn't realize the strength of the mother character as I did, and I knew that if I brought the mother in and made her the hinge on which everything swung, the book would be a story. It would work as a book. I told Tom that's what I intended to do . . .

I decided that although nobody's life makes any sense, if you're going to make a book out of it you might as well make it into a story. I remember saying to my wife, "I am now going upstairs to invent the story of my life." And I started writing, on the days when I wasn't doing my newspaper column, and I rewrote that whole book—almost the entire thing—in about six months. That was the book that was eventually published.

That account by Russell Baker not only led me to the title *Inventing the Truth*—perhaps the best possible title for a book about memoir. It states the most important principle for writing the story of your life: mere facts aren't enough. No matter how many details you diligently collect about the people and places and events in your past, they won't add up to a memoir. You must make a narrative arrangement.

We like to think that an interesting life will simply fall into place on the page. It won't; life is too disorganized. We like to think that Thoreau went home to Concord and just wrote up his notes. He didn't. He wrote seven drafts of *Walden* in eight years, piecing together by what Margaret Fuller called the mosaic method a book that seems casual and even chatty. Thoreau wasn't a woodsman when he went to the woods; he was a writer, and he wrote one of our sacred texts.

To write a memoir you must manufacture a text. You must construct a narrative so compelling that readers will want to keep reading. You must, in short, practice a craft. You can never forget the storyteller's ancient rules of maintaining tension and momentum—rules you've known in your bones since you were a child listening to bedtime stories.

You can also never forget that you are the protagonist in your story. Not the hero; most writers are uncomfortable with that idea—they weren't trying to be a hero and they don't feel like a hero. But you are the central actor in your story, and you must give yourself a plot. If Russell Baker did any "inventing" when he rewrote *Growing Up* it was perhaps to alter a time sequence, or to collapse several events into one event, or to heighten a personality trait. But he didn't violate the truth; his memoir rings absolutely true. Like a playwright or a screenwriter, he rearranged and compressed his story to give it dramatic shape. You must also find your story's narrative line.

How should you begin? As always, that's the horrible problem. You've found that old trunk with all the letters and postcards and photographs and diaries, the school and college yearbooks, the football programs and ticket stubs, the wedding announcements and baby shower invitations. Your life is there waiting for you in scraps of paper and scraps of memory. Now all you have to do is put it together.

Many people of a certain age, feeling a first twinge of mortality or arthritis, have asked my advice on how to write a memoir. What I tell them isn't what they expect to hear, because we're starting from different assumptions. They assume that they should start at the beginning ("I was born") and summarize the high points of their life in chronological order. I don't think writing works that way, especially memoir. It doesn't follow the road maps we make in advance.

Here's the advice I give:

Go to your desk on Monday morning and think of some event that's unusually vivid in your memory: your first day at summer camp, your senior prom, your high school graduation, an encounter with a teacher, an athletic contest, a music recital, the day you joined the army, the birth of a child, a moment of triumph, a moment of humiliation, a moment of love. Any event will do as long as you still remember it vividly.

Call that memory back and write it up. Describe what happened and how you felt about it. What you write doesn't have to be long: one page, two pages, five pages. But the episode should be complete in itself: one story with a beginning and an end. When you finish it, put what you've written in a manila folder and get on with your life: go to work, take a walk, pick up the kids.

On Tuesday morning, do it again. Tuesday's memory doesn't need to be related to Monday's memory. If you wrote on Monday about your first day in the army, what you write on Tuesday doesn't have to be about your second day in the army. It might be some incident that happened when you were eight years old. Take whatever memory comes knocking. Put entirely out of your mind the idea that you're embarking on a longer project: a memoir, an article, a book. Write up Tuesday's memory and put it in the folder.

Do that every day—preferably, at the same time of day. After a while the entries will begin to add up. They may not fall into any relationship with each other, but they're doing useful work. First, you're exercising new muscles: memory muscles, writing muscles, organizing muscles. Second, you're discovering that the subconscious mind plays a big role in this kind of writing. While you slept, your subconscious mind didn't. It was busy poking around in all those memories you stirred up, dredging up other moments in your past.

Keep this up for two months, or three months. Don't fidget. Don't be impatient to start writing your "memoir"— the one you had in mind before you began. Then, one day, take all your entries out of the folder and spread them out on the floor. (Vladimir Nabokov once told an interviewer that he wrote his books on three-by-five index cards, in no particular order.) Here are some of the things you'll discover.

You'll discover that your first entries are quite stiff and self-conscious. That's natural. All of us who write need a certain amount of time, often quite a lot of time, to relax and find our natural voice. Therefore you'll notice that the entries you wrote in the second month are warmer than the ones you wrote in the first month, which are a little wooden, a little impersonal, a little pretentious, a little looking-over-your-shoulder to see who's watching. You may never use much of what you wrote in the first month. But that writing wasn't wasted. You couldn't have arrived at the confidence of the second month without doing the stretching exercises of the first month.

So you'll gradually begin to find your style—the person you want to sound like, the person you really are. If you don't find that person, you won't write a memoir that anyone will want to read. All writing is talking to someone else on paper. Talk like yourself.

You'll make similar discoveries in the area of content. Certain themes and patterns will emerge in what you've written. Your material will begin to tell you: "This is a good direction and a good voice. It's true, it's funny, it's interesting. Stay with it." It will also tell you: "This is not interesting. It's not as interesting as you thought it was. In fact, it's pretty boring." Or it will tell you: "This is a digression. It's not relevant to the main thread of your narrative." In short, you'll begin to glimpse what your memoir is really about. And what it's *not* about. That's also a crucial thing to learn, as Annie Dillard points out in *Inventing the Truth*, describing how she wrote her memoir about growing up in Pittsburgh, *An American Childhood*:

In the course of writing this memoir I've learned all sorts of things, quite inadvertently, about myself and about various relationships. But these things are not important to the book, and I easily leave them out. I leave out many things that were important to my life but of no concern for the book, like the summer I spent in

Wyoming when I was fifteen. I keep the action in Pittsburgh. I see no reason to drag everybody off to Wyoming just because I want to tell them about my summer vacation. You have to take pains in a memoir not to hang on the reader's arm like a drunk and say, "And then I did this and it was so interesting."

One way to think about Dillard's point—what to leave out—is to keep your unities intact. In this case it's unity of place. Dillard decided that her memoir was about her childhood in Pittsburgh; therefore she eliminates everything that didn't happen in Pittsburgh. Vivian Gornick's *Fierce Attachments* is about growing up in the Bronx; Samuel Hynes' *The Growing Seasons* is about growing up in Minneapolis; Andre Aciman's *Out of Egypt* is about growing up in Alexandria. When I think of those books I see those places and hear their voices and smell their smells. Don't drag us off to Wyoming if Pittsburgh is your story.

O.K. Now all you have to do is start. Please trust the process. If the process is sound, the product will take care of itself.

Inventing the Truth was popular with writers and teachers because it was specific and anecdotal, and in 1995 the publisher asked if I would prepare an expanded second edition by adding new writers. I liked the idea of broadening the book to include types of memoir that hadn't been represented in the first edition, and I invited four men and women who had written memoirs of unusual breadth and texture. To preserve the oral integrity of the book I went to them with my tape recorder and then edited the stories they told me.

Eileen Simpson represented all the memoir writers who incur what they know will be considerable pain to repossess their past. For *Poets in Their Youth*, a memoir of her life with her first husband, John Berryman, and his famously self-destructive fellow poets, Simpson had to revisit the collapse of that marriage and of the dazzling world it was built on. To write *Orphans*, which recalls her upbringing without parents, she did historical research on orphanhood that became so traumatic that she had to abandon the book several times. For *Reversals* she had to reveal the lifelong shame, carefully hidden as an adult, of having been a dyslexic child, the class dunce, unable to read, in the days before dyslexia was understood. What saved her in each case was the knowledge, learned in her later career as a psychotherapist, that the past is better confronted than avoided—a valuable lesson for all memoirists fearful of opening Pandora's box. Simpson even used her therapist's technique on herself, lying on a couch to summon back a weekend party 30 years earlier with the poet Robert Lowell and the writer Jean Stafford. "It was like waiting under water for a certain species of fish to swim by," she says.

Ian Frazier represented all the writers—you may be one of them—who inherit a vast hoard of family papers and mementos going back many generations and who wonder how they can possibly weed it all out and shape it into a coherent story. Frazier began working on his book *Family* after his parents died within a year of each other, leaving an apartment in Ohio in which nothing had been thrown away. "Objects suggest narrative," Frazier told me, and for two and a half years he dug like a paleontologist through his parents' hundreds of letters and artifacts—old neckties and purses and theater programs and navy ID cards—"to infer the culture they came from and its plot" and thereby give meaning to their lives. He soon realized that those lives could only be given meaning within the context of the long decline of the Protestant establishment and its values. That gave him a second plot, intertwined with the first, and deflected him down many overgrown trails of 19th-century American social history. "It's like building a house," he said. "You get to a certain part and you realize that you need a different gauge of lumber or something, and you have to go get it."

Henry Louis Gates, Jr., chairman of the African-American Studies Department at Harvard, represented all the writers who use memoir to record what it's like to belong to a minority culture in America. His *Colored People*, recalling his boyhood in Piedmont, West Virginia, is pungently honest about how that black community went about its living and its loving. "I wanted to write a book that imitated the specialness of black culture when no white people are around," Gates told me, noting that earlier black authors like Richard Wright and Ralph Ellison edited out of their work all such rollicking details that whites could use against their race. "That's totally bogus," Gates said. "If I had thought I was writing for middle-class ladies with white gloves on I couldn't have written this book." His is the first generation of black American males, he said, secure enough to write a memoir without kowtowing to an imagined censor. "If you ask me what the legacy of my book will be, I would like it to make younger people freer to tell their own stories."

My fourth new writer, Jill Ker Conway, represented a type of memoir that never loses its appeal: growing up in a faraway place. In *The Road from Coorain* she recalls the isolated girlhood she spent on a sheep station in the Australian outback, the seven-year drought that killed her parents' homesteading dream and ended up killing her father, and the ordeal of escaping from a suffocating male society and starting over in America. Hers is also a strongly feminist memoir. Conway describes how she rebelled against the "romantic plot" that women had traditionally acted out, acquiescing in seeing themselves as passive players in somebody else's story—even strong women like her heroine, the reformer Jane Addams. "I thought it was important," she told me, "to relate the story of a young woman taking charge of her own life in an unromantic way, in which it's perfectly clear that she arrives at a moment of choice."

Women have been so unassertive about their identity, Conway said, that in the 20th century eight autobiographies were written by men for every one written by a woman. That kind of imbalance was one of my reasons for wanting Conway and Gates in the second edition of *Inventing the Truth*. Both of them write boldly as outsiders who freed themselves from an unequal system. You, too can use writing to break out of society's confining boxes. Be true to the culture you were born into. Have the courage to tell your story as only you can tell it.

So *Inventing the Truth* went out into the world again. But a funny thing happened to memoir while nobody was looking: it was getting a bad name. Talk shows on cable television spawned a national appetite for true confession in the mid-1990s and swept away all the old codes of civility and taste. The result was an avalanche of memoirs that were little more than therapy, the authors bashing their parents and siblings and exulting in the lurid details of their tussle with drink, drug addiction, anorexia, obesity, co-dependency, depression, attempted suicide and other talk-show syndromes. Those chronicles of victimhood were the dark side of the personal narrative boom. If memoir had become mere self-indulgence, a medium for reprisal and settling old grievances—so the argument went—it must be a degraded genre.

Amid so much derision, what were serious memoir writers supposed to think? In 1998 I prepared a third edition of *Inventing the Truth*, with Frank McCourt added to the lineup, and in my new introduction I tried to answer that question and suggest some guidelines:

The marvel of Frank McCourt's childhood is that he survived it, as he himself notes in the third sentence of his book. The second marvel is that he was able to triumph over it in *Angela's Ashes*, beating back the past with grace and humor and with the power of language. Those same qualities are at the heart of all the good memoirs of the 1990s—books such as Pete Hamill's *A Drinking Life* and Mary Karr's *The Liars' Club* and Tobias Wolff's *This Boy's Life*. Anyone might think the domestic chaos and alcoholism and violence that enveloped those writers when they were young would have long since hardened the heart. Both Karr and Wolff were lugged around the country by barely competent mothers running from unstable males and taking up with men who were even worse—nightmarish new stepfathers for children whose own fathers had forsaken them. Yet they look back with compassion . . . If these books by McCourt, Hamill, Karr and Wolff represent the new memoir at its best, it's because they were written with love. They elevate the pain of the past with forgiveness, arriving at a larger truth about families in various stages of brokenness. There's no self-pity, no whining, no hunger for revenge; the authors are as honest about their own young selves as they are about the sins of their elders. We are not victims, they want us to know. We come from a tribe of fallible people, prisoners of our own destructiveness, and we have endured to tell the story without judgment and to get on with our lives.

Whether the authors of certain recent memoirs *ought* to have written those books, breaking powerful taboos and social covenants, isn't the point. When Kathryn Harrison wrote *The Kiss*, a memoir about her affair with her father, the critics devoted so much space to scolding her and telling her she had violated the privacy of her children—which was none of their business—that they hardly got around to discussing her book.

The only pertinent question about any memoir is: is it a good book or a bad book? If you use memoir to look for your own humanity and the humanity of the people who crossed your life, however much pain they caused you, readers will connect with your journey. What they won't connect with is whining. Dispose of that anger somewhere else. Get your intention clear before you start and tell your story with integrity.

11.

Writing as a Ministry

ONE DAY IN 1992 I got a call from the dean of the Earlham School of Religion, a division of Earlham College, a Quaker college in Indiana. He told me that his school was establishing a program called "The Ministry of Writing," and he asked if I would give the keynote talk. I said I would like nothing better. Then I asked: "How did you know?" How did he know that I've always regarded my writing as a form of ministry? I had never told anyone; I thought that would be presumptuous. He said, "It's all through your work."

That puzzled me, because it's not all through my work—not, at least, overtly. God turns up occasionally as a governing presence, and my sentences take some of their cadences and allusions from the King James Bible. But there's no mention of religious worship or religious belief—the residue of all those Sunday mornings spent in Protestant churches singing the hymns, reciting the Psalms and listening to the Word.

Yet on second thought I saw that the dean had me pegged. As a writer I try to operate within a framework of Christian principles, and the words that are important to me are religious words: witness, pilgrimage, intention. I think of intention as the writer's soul. Writers can write to affirm and to celebrate, or they can write to debunk and to destroy; the choice is ours. Editors may ask us to do destructive work for some purpose of their own, but nobody can make us write what we don't want to write. We get to keep intention.

I always write to affirm—or, if I start negatively, deploring some situation or trend that strikes me as injurious, my goal is to arrive at a constructive point. I choose to write about people whose values I respect and who do life-affirming work; my pleasure is to bear witness to their lives. Much of my writing has taken the form of a pilgrimage: to sacred places that represent the best of America, to musicians and other artists who represent the best of their art.

My mother came from a long line of devout Maine and Connecticut Yankees, and she thought it was a Christian obligation to be cheerful. It is because of her that I am cursed with optimism. The belief that I can somehow will things to go right more often than they go wrong—or to be an agent of God's intention for them to go right—has brought many adjectives down on my head, none of them flattering: naive, credulous, simple-minded. All true. I plead guilty to positive thinking.

Whether this is a religious position I'll leave to some theologian. In any case, it's an act of faith—a challenge hurled in the face of the cynics. I like St. Paul's admonition: "Be not forgetful to entertain strangers: for thereby some have entertained angels unawares." I'm far more often surprised by grace than disappointed. I see too much goodness in everyday life, too many men and women and children going about God's work, not to want to hitch myself to that enterprise.

My attraction to subjects that involve a pilgrimage has often put me in the presence of a sacramental moment. I think of a Bedouin family in the Sahara Desert near Timbuktu—a family with almost no possessions—who made me a gift of hospitality I've never forgotten. I think of the Vietnamese poet in Hanoi, Duong Tuong, whose poem "At the Vietnam Wall" was a gift of reconciliation that as an American I never expected to deserve.

I think of a Balinese drummer who came into my life without warning one night in 1952. My job as drama editor of the *Herald Tribune* required me to attend every Broadway opening, and I was sitting in the Fulton Theater waiting for a show called "Dancers of Bali" to begin. I had no idea what to expect; nowhere had my life or my education been touched by the cultures of Southeast Asia. The curtain went up and I heard a CLANG! that almost knocked me out of my seat. Twenty-five Balinese men were sitting cross-legged on the stage, striking an assortment of cymbals and gongs and xylophones with an intricacy of rhythm unlike anything I had ever heard. It was my first gamelan orchestra. Where had this wonderful sound been all my life? Although the scale had only five tones, the notes rose and fell in cascades of melody and counterpoint, sometimes reaching high intensity, sometimes turning slow and delicate. Yet no sign ever seemed to pass between the musicians and the dignified older man playing a large drum who was obviously their leader.

I was further electrified when the dancers began to appear, costumed as princes and demons and dragons, presenting a succession of temple dances. They had an elegance of body movement and hand gesture that was new to me, and the program concluded with a classical *legong*, performed by three lithe little girls who were tightly wrapped in sarongs and seemed to have no bones. I learned from the *Playbill* that the troupe was from one village, called Peliatan, but that what I had seen was not unlike what I might see in any Balinese village. Art in Bali was an assumed possession; the language didn't even have a word for "art."

That was something I wanted to see, and the next summer I traveled to Indonesia and went to Bali and drove up into the hills to Peliatan and looked up the old drummer, whose name was Anak Agung Gde Madera. (Anak Agung is a princely title.) He told me that the troupe was not long back from its successful tour of America; they had played 14 cities. I asked him where the musicians and dancers were now. He said they were all back at their jobs, mostly in the rice fields. Would they be performing anywhere? Not this week; no temple dances were scheduled on Peliatan's religious calendar. I should try some other village.

That's when I learned the first rule of traveling in Bali: ask and you will hear about a temple ceremony somewhere. Village X is doing a *barong* this evening, Village Y is doing a *baris* and a *kebyar* tomorrow. Night after night I sat in the courtyard of some Balinese village and watched the same dances I had seen on Broadway, exquisitely performed and accompanied on a full gamelan by men and women who during the day had been laborers. Children and chickens were everywhere. Mothers stood in a circle, holding their babies. The tales from the *Ramayana* and the movements of the dancers and the tinkling of the gamelan got absorbed almost from birth. Another CLANG! went off in my head. I saw that religion and art were intertwined with life, not taught in separate buildings and special classrooms on designated days of the week, as they were in my culture. I envied that unity, and after that I began to look for it in all my travels. I've felt the spirit at work in villages in Africa and Asia and Brazil where nothing in my genes or my upbringing had prepared me for that experience.

In 1972 I went back to Bali, this time with Caroline, and we headed up to Peliatan. I wanted to find out whether the Anak Agung was still alive. I asked some village boys, and they led us to a pavilion, and there he was, teaching the *legong* to a class of little girls. Twenty years had turned him gray, and he moved with the stiffness of old age. But he greeted me warmly, and we talked about the long-ago night on Broadway that had brought me to his village once before. Then he went back to work.

He lifted one of the little girls and put her down so that her feet were on his feet, facing forward. Then he held her by her skinny wrists and began to perform the *legong*, humming the gamelan melody for that portion of the dance. Back and forth and sideways they moved in stylized steps, bending and leaning, starting and stopping, the girl's tiny feet riding wherever the big feet took her. I could almost feel the rhythms being passed from one body to the other; the old man's face was so serious and so tender. Then he gave the same lesson to the other little girls. They were all as serious as he was; there was no sense that this was a chore, or extra homework, or anything but life itself. It was the best lesson I ever saw.

But it's not necessary to go to Bali or Hanoi or Timbuktu. In America I've found just as many manifestations of grace. In 1990 I went to Montgomery, Alabama, to write about the newly dedicated memorial by Maya Lin to the men, women and children who were killed during the struggle for civil rights. The piece would be a chapter in my book *American Places*, a pilgrimage to 15 iconic or inspirational American sites.

Maya Lin's earlier Vietnam Memorial, in Washington, was, to me, one of America's religious places. With that wall of incised names she enabled the American people to heal through their fingertips the wounds of a war that had torn the nation apart. Now she had turned her mind and her heart to the dead of the civil rights era, one of America's great religious movements, its roots going back to the early-19th-century abolitionists, its prophet the great religious writer Abraham Lincoln. To this day Lincoln's Second Inaugural Address, echoing with wrathful Old and New Testament phrases, serving notice that the Civil War would end only when God wanted it to end ("the Almighty has His own purposes"), speaks to the sin of slavery in language more powerful than that of any American writer.

In Montgomery I was glad to find Maya Lin's memorial only a few blocks from the Dexter Avenue Baptist Church, where a 25-year-old preacher, Martin Luther King, Jr., started it all. The memorial has two components. One is a wall of water falling over the words that King paraphrased from the Book of Amos in two historic speeches—his "I have a dream" speech in Washington and his speech at the start of the Montgomery bus boycott: "We will not be satisfied until justice rolls down like waters and righteousness like a mighty stream."

The other component is a large circular table of black granite. Carved into its top, around the perimeter, are 53 chronological entries naming and identifying people who were murdered in the South in the 1950s and '60s—the four young girls, for instance, who were bombed in a Birmingham church and the 14-year-old Emmett Till, who was killed for speaking to a white woman in Mississippi. A thin film of water flows over the tabletop. Most visitors walk slowly around the table, pausing to read and touch the names of the dead just beneath the water.

Afterward I asked Maya Lin how the idea for the memorial occurred to her. For several months, she told me, no ideas came at all. "The discipline is to not jump too fast," she said. "If you jump to a form too quickly it won't have the understood meaning you want for it." Finally the day arrived for her to fly to Montgomery to inspect the site, and it was on the plane, reading a book called *Eyes on the Prize*, that she came upon King's phrase about justice rolling down.

"The minute I hit that quote," she said, "I knew that the whole piece had to be about water." What she didn't anticipate was the power that words would generate when they were combined with water. "At the dedication ceremony," she told me, "I was moved when people started to cry. Emmett Till's mother was touching his name beneath the water and crying, and I realized that her tears were becoming part of the memorial."

Did Maya Lin describe that sacramental moment to any other writer? Did any other writer see the old Balinese drummer giving a *legong* lesson? Probably not. Why was I the chosen witness? Mathematically, the odds favored my being there. Writers who go on spiritual quests put themselves in a position to observe spiritual transactions. But I could also argue that I was put there by God—a God who wants to make sure his best stories get told.

Most people are on some kind of pilgrimage, whether or not they recognize it as such. If you put your writing in the form of a quest you will make a connection with your readers that will surprise you with its power.

One more sacramental moment.

My class at Princeton, the class of 1944, was a wartime class—and always would be. We were defined by World War II. We had come to college in the fall of 1940, carefree young men who thought the world would never change. Then, on December 7, 1941, only a few months into our sophomore year, it changed.

The Japanese attack on Pearl Harbor threw the campus into stunned confusion. Nobody knew what to do; the first impulse was to run out and enlist. A week later the president of Princeton, Harold W. Dodds, called the whole university together in Alexander Hall, one of those Victorian Gothic monstrosities that adorn every college of a certain age. President Dodds told us he had been in touch with "Washington." Washington said it had its hands full and didn't need us right away. Washington wanted us to stay in college and get educated for "the war effort"—at least for now. I can still hear the hush in that auditorium as we strained to hear the words that held our fate.

Through the winter, spring and summer of 1942 we took courses that were compressed and elided, like a speeded-up movie; we were amassing wisdom, which Washington, in its own wisdom, would use to smash the Axis. But the great disconnection had begun. Every week more students and professors leached away into the armed forces. The texture of college life unraveled, and eventually 82 percent of our class—562 men—went off to war. After the war, Humpty-Dumpty never quite got put back together again. Too much glue had been lost.

In the spring of 1994 I went to Normandy to write an article about the 50th anniversary of D-Day. I was making a pilgrimage to the day that was the turning point of the war that scattered our class. I decided to focus on the American military cemetery, which sits on a bluff above Omaha Beach, the beach that American troops took with severe losses on June 6, 1944. I had heard that the cemetery was a place of unusual power. I wanted to know how that power exerts itself on the people who come there as visitors.

From the moment I arrived I knew I was in the presence of something that had been done right. This was landscape architecture distilled to its purest elements: earth, sea and sky. The 9,386 white marble crosses, perfectly erect and perfectly aligned, are on a tract of land that is perfectly sited, high above Omaha Beach. (On Jewish graves the crosses are capped by a Star of David). Just enough trees have been planted, but not too many; the usual funerary custom is to smother grief in greenery. Instead my eye was freed to concentrate on the great simplicities: immaculate grass, white crosses that have a plain dignity, two American flags flying from tall flagpoles, and a tremendous sky. Beyond, the English Channel extends the view to the horizon.

This burial ground for American soldiers is visited by almost two million people a year, most of them Europeans. "It's reassuring to them," the superintendent, Joseph Rivers, told me. "They look at all those headstones and think, 'They did it for us.' For young French people D-Day was the day their grandparents were liberated. The news that 'the Allies have landed in Normandy' was like a beacon in the sky. It must have been the most uplifting thing."

Rivers is a custodian, above all, of memory. "Just this week," he said, "I got letters from students in Sweden, Italy and Brazil asking for more information. That happens a lot after they visit the cemetery. The student from Sweden asked if I could give her the name of an American veteran who fought here. She wanted to correspond with him and find out what the invasion was like for someone her age: 'How did it help or disturb you?' 'Did it make you a better person?' 'What was your life like afterward?' Young people ask that kind of question. To me their curiosity is comforting because Europeans don't teach their history, or they hide it. These students say they were never given the amplitude of what happened here."

I began to understand the power I had come looking for. The cemetery is infinitely useful. It serves whatever emotional needs are brought to it. Its most merciful gift is the gift of absolution. Joseph Rivers told me about one recent visitor, a man who had seen action on D-Day with a naval combat demolition unit, clearing mines and other underwater hazards.

"He was my first 'NCDU,' " Rivers said. "We almost never get one of those. I met him walking among the graves with his two grown grandsons, who were doctors, and he was very tense, very nervous. He had blocked out the whole D-Day experience. He said, 'My wife didn't want to hear about it, and my in-laws didn't want to hear about it, so I've been passive about the whole thing.' Suddenly he opened up—for the first time in almost fifty years. It all started coming back to him in a flash. His grandsons stared at him in amazement; they had never seen that grandfather before. He just had to get it out. And as he talked, his whole frame of mind altered. He said it felt good, and he realized that he had had a satisfying life. The cemetery changed his whole outlook."

Rivers and his cemetery stayed with me long after I got home. I assumed that my generation of men had made its peace with World War II; I didn't expect those years to have been withheld from wives and children for half a century. But when I told friends about the NCDU who finally spilled everything, they weren't surprised. Several middle-aged women said their fathers never revealed what they did and what they thought during the war. Those daughters felt that this was not only a deprivation for the men; they themselves felt deprived of knowing something important about their fathers. They resented having been left out.

All these emotions came crowding back in early June when I went to Princeton for my 50th reunion, one of life's summarizing events. By a potent coincidence, the reunion fell on the same weekend as the 50th anniversary of D-Day. All week long the invasion of Normandy had been replayed in the media; we heard it coming. The memory of June 6, 1944, was part of the baggage we all brought with us.

I had never been much of a reunion-goer, partly because our class had been dispersed before it had a chance to become a class. But on this Friday night I felt that something beyond obligation and loyalty was drawing us back. The reunion began with a class dinner, and I scanned the faces of the old men in the 1944 tent, delving for some trace of a person I might have known as a freshman or a sophomore. Many of them, however, were strangers. Yet a large number seemed to be back. Later we would learn that the class broke Princeton's all-time record for 50th-reunion attendance and also for the size of the class gift, both in dollars and in ratio; 85.4 percent of the class participated. That surprised me. Had the war that pulled us apart become the bond that was pulling us together?

The main event of the reunion was a gathering on Saturday morning in Alexander Hall, the auditorium where the whole class had last been together, one week after Pearl

Harbor. Most of us were accompanied by our wives. Matrimony, that much-defamed institution, never looked better; many of those marriages began as dates on the Princeton campus in the early 1940s. Caroline had never been to a reunion with me. I told her I didn't want to do this one alone.

Alexander Hall had been handsomely refurbished, but I'm sure I wasn't the only one who felt old emanations from under the new paint. The ghost of Harold Dodds was perched somewhere in the rafters. Princeton's president had won our affection during the long war by sending periodic form letters to everyone who had gone into the armed forces, telling us we were not forgotten. One year he enclosed a list of 100 Modern Library titles and said the university would send us any three books, wherever we were. I got my *Don Quixote* in a sand-blown tent near the Algerian town of Blida. Shakespeare's plays caught up with me in a snow-blown tent near the Italian town of Brindisi.

Four of us had been asked to give brief talks reflecting on some aspect of the American experience as it pertained to the class of 1944. As the first speaker, I thought I should address the historical event that gave us our collective identity, and I spoke about the trip I had just made to the cemetery at Omaha Beach. I described its perfect location high above the English Channel and its perfect rows of white crosses. I described the European visitors who say "They did it for us" and the NCDU who had repressed his memories, ending with these words of Joseph Rivers: "When American veterans who fought in Normandy come here they see that America has given nobility to the men who died, and that relieves some of their survivors' guilt. Most people don't give themselves a long-range destiny; life is kind of a rambling thing. But here they look at these graves and it hits them: 'Those men died for a set of values, and they *still* represent those values. Those men did something very unselfish.' "

The stillness in Alexander Hall as I described the cemetery to my classmates—and to their wives and children and grandchildren—was a presence in itself, filling every crevice. The absolving cemetery had extended its blessing to us all.

The last of the morning's speakers was Hervey Stockman, a fighter pilot who saw action in all of the class's hot and cold wars: World War II, Korea, the first U-2 flight over the Soviet Union, and Vietnam, where his plane crashed and he spent six years in a seven-by-seven-foot prison cell in Hanoi. He had been reluctant to talk about that ordeal, but the class officers asked him to try, feeling that in his character and his generous heart he represented the best of what the class of 1944 set out so long ago to be.

"Preparing these words was like visiting an old, untended graveyard," Hervey Stockman said, looking out at us from the lectern, a trim man with a warm smile. He began by recalling the brutal treatment he received in the early months of his imprisonment: "I was a foul, decrepit wreck of a man." Then he described the slow process by which "my mind was awakened and reunited to my body and I had the will to live and regain my strength." He spoke slowly, barely controlling his emotions, but without self-pity, and when he walked back to his seat, his slightly stiff gait betraying his long captivity, the class rose in an ovation that had no relation to the applause usually heard at the end of a speech: mere hand clapping. It had tremendous solemnity—it was emotional without being sentimental—and it rumbled through the auditorium. Most of us were crying or reaching for a handkerchief. Caroline later said she had never seen men cry so comfortably. In that moment we were healed.

And then it was over, and we were back out in the warm sunshine of the campus, enjoying a lighthearted lunch and enjoying each other's company. Afterward we gathered in front of Nassau Hall for the annual "P-rade" of reunion classes. I couldn't help remembering that I first marched in that parade as a small boy, wearing the orange-and-black jacket of my father's class of 1909. Now, when the band struck up a medley of Princeton marches I could hear my father singing those songs to me as an even smaller boy, hardly out of the crib. They are almost the first songs I can remember.

12.

Recovering the Past

ONE DAY IN 1999 a man named Bill Lehren came to my office in New York, carrying a large package carefully tied with string. He had called to tell me what he wanted to show me, and I could hardly wait for him to get it unwrapped. He put the package on my desk and went to work, tugging at the knots and removing the paper with slow and almost liturgical motions. Finally the object was revealed: the mechanical baseball game that consumed thousands of hours of my boyhood. I hadn't seen one in more than 60 years.

Bill Lehren's visit closed a circle that first opened on April 6, 1983, when I wrote an article about that same game in the *New York Times*. Video games were then a new craze, and there was much ululation in the land over how America's young people were squandering their youth in video arcades. I wanted to point out that my own boyhood addiction to this particular baseball game had been no less obsessive and that it didn't seem to have ruined me.

For a boy growing up in the 1930s, I explained, it wasn't easy to gratify a craving for baseball. Television didn't exist, and games on the radio were scarce. Manufacturers of board games tried to cater to the need, but theirs were dismal products, dependent on some numerical indicator—dice or cards or the spin of a wheel—to determine what was happening on the "field." They didn't convey any sense of the real game, or even require skill.

Then, one year, I found under the Christmas tree a baseball game that looked and acted like a baseball game. The field was a sheet of green metal, roughly two feet square, enclosed by a low wooden fence. The nine players—little cast-iron men—stood at their positions around the diamond. In front of every player was an indented pocket. If a ball was hit at a player, it would bounce off him into the pocket for an out. Otherwise it would roll to parts of the field designated "foul," "single," "double," "triple" or "home run."

The bat was powered by a tightly coiled spring. When it was released it swung fiercely across the plate. The boy who was the batter, kneeling behind home plate, held the bat back, waiting for the pitch. The boy who was the pitcher, kneeling at the opposite end, kept his fingers on two buttons, one on each side, which controlled the pitches. By pressing them in different ways he could pitch a fast ball, a slow ball or several intermediate speeds. Thus the classic duel between batter and pitcher was preserved with all its rewards and indignities. The batter, anticipating a fast ball, would release the bat before a slow ball arrived. Or, expecting a slow ball, he would hold the bat back and watch the ball shoot past him into the catcher's pocket. But the batter could also guess right. That this ancient battle of wits could be replicated in a child's toy struck me as a marvel of invention.

The game gave itself to those who took time to get in tune with its soul. There was no question of my not taking enough time; the game altered the whole concept of leisure for me and my friend Charlie Willis. Nor did it occur to us to play on a one-to-one basis; Charlie was the New York Yankees and I was the Detroit Tigers. Summers turned to winters and back to other summers, and still the rivalry went on. Mountains of paper—box scores, batting averages, team statistics—joined the big-league gum cards and old issues of *Baseball* magazine in the rising litter of my room. I still remember one day when Charlie and I played 22 games.

"I sometimes wonder what became of my game," I wrote at the end of my article. "My mother must have thrown it away when I went into the army. I've never seen it at any of those antique shows that sell old mechanical banks and toys, and I can't recall who made it. But in the mists of memory I see the word WOLVERINE. What 'Rosebud' was to Citizen Kane, 'Wolverine' is to me—a clue almost irrecoverably faint. I mention it in case anyone finds the game in an attic or a basement or a garage. I can be there on the next plane—and so can Charlie Willis."

It only took a few days for the letters to start trickling in. "Destiny must have been guiding my actions yesterday," wrote L. Robert Feitig, of Stroudsburg, Pennsylvania, "as I went to pick up my *Philadelphia Inquirer*. As Fate would dictate, the newsstand was out of the *Inquirer*, so I purchased a *New York Times*, something I rarely do. There before my eyes was your article. I too, spent many hours on the floor, playing that game with my boyhood chum, Jim Sutch. I still have the game, and have played it with two more generations, my son John and now my three grandsons. They are still rather young, and as a result they have trouble hitting the fast ball and complain when I shoot it past them, but they will soon learn how to hit it."

The name and maker of the game were provided by J. M. Pittman, of North Bellmore, New York. "You will be pleased to know," he wrote, "that at least one of Wolverine Supply & Manufacturing Company's 'Pennant Winner' baseball games still exists. My brother and I received our game at Christmas, 1932. It was purchased from the old Frederick Loeser store in Brooklyn. We, too, organized leagues, had pennant winners, an All-Star game each season, and of course a World Series. My notebooks contain line scores and averages and statistics of more than 1,000 games. There are records of pitching duels between Lefty Grove and Carl Hubbell, Dizzy Dean and Lon Warneke, as well as games broken up by the bats of Jimmy Foxx, Al Simmons, Lou Gehrig and Babe Ruth."

Fredric Kolb, of Bernardsville, New Jersey, wrote: "I, too, went through many of the experiences you describe, especially all those board games. Then, in 1929, my Dad purchased the Wolverine baseball game at A. G. Spalding, in New York. It cost $15, which was a vast sum in those days. I started a league with three other boys, and one of them produced a newspaper each Saturday with reports and averages of all our games. That first year I won the league championship on the final day of the season. The other boys soon realized my 'home field' advantage, and two of them received games of their own the next Christmas. Each of them began to 'doctor' their game by adjusting the pitching springs, bat tension, etc., to their own advantage. How much like the real game!"

That authenticity was also recalled by George Culver, of Massapequa, New York, who said, "That game completely captivated me back in 1936. The amazing thing was that the inventor was able to keep the hits and the scores to just about what you'd expect in a real game." The largest league was reported by Lou Sanders, of Mineola, New York. "In my neighborhood," he wrote, "there were 12 fellows, each one representing a major league team and each player keeping his own lineup and statistics."

Two mothers, like mine, figured in speculation about the disposal of the game itself. "I just found my game in my mother's attic," wrote Ian G. MacDonald of Beacon, New York. "It was missing the men, but they're probably hidden in a 'safe place.' A 'safe place' in my mother's house is equivalent to a black hole." Frank E. Darnulc, of Suffern, New York, wrote: "I also was the happy owner of that game. My mother was great on getting rid of things not used every day, and I suppose the game went down the dumbwaiter."

The last letter was postmarked Booneville, Arkansas, and I could hardly believe the return address: WOLVERINE TOY COMPANY. It was from William W. Lehren, vice president of sales. "By the time I reached the third paragraph of your article," he said, "I couldn't help but think, 'If only he had seen our Pennant Winner baseball game.' I was covered with goose flesh as I read the remainder of the piece. Wolverine is a medium-sized toy manufacturer with a low profile. We made the Pennant Winner from 1929 to 1950. When I joined the company in 1948 it was considered a rather high-priced carriage-trade item. Unfortunately it required demonstration, and the product was dropped. After reading your article we dug around in our museum and found that we had one game in our inventory. Needless to say, it will not be allowed off the premises. However, if you or Charlie Willis ever happen to be in this vicinity I'd love to take you on for a few games."

That was the same game that the same Bill Lehren had just unwrapped in my office in New York. He had bought it from the company when he retired to Connecticut. Wolverine, he told me, was founded in 1903, in Pittsburgh, by a die maker and metal fabricator from Michigan named Benjamin Franklin Bain, who named his company for the University of Michigan football team. The business thrived by making products like pie tins and stovetop toasters for America's kitchens.

Around 1910, Bain was asked to make dies for a gravity-action toy to be called Sandy Andy, which consisted of a cart that got pulled by a counterweight to the top of an incline, where it received a load of sand from a hopper. Its weight then took it back down and it dumped its load. After Bain's dies were made, the inventor went broke. Bain decided he might as well go ahead and manufacture Sandy Andy in his own factory—a decision that would result in one of the most enduring of metal toys. Wolverine made Sandy Andy well into the 1950s and even sold a box of sand to go with it—an accessory that parents may not have appreciated having around the house.

In 1914, Bill Lehren's father, James Lehren, a young immigrant from Holland, got part-time work as a demonstrator of Sandy Andy at Gimbel's department store in New York. He did so well that he was hired by the company to come to Pittsburgh as its only salesman. After Bain died the company faltered and was near death when James Lehren took over as president in 1928. He steered Wolverine through the Depression and World War II, when the metal factory was converted to making military equipment.

"I joined Wolverine as a salesman and became vice president in the mid-1960s," Bill Lehren told me. "In 1968 the company was sold to a private conglomerate and moved to Booneville, Arkansas. We shipped a whole barge load of punch presses and other metal-working machinery there from Pittsburgh—down the Ohio and the Mississippi and up the Arkansas River. Later the woman who was president of Wolverine decided it was improper for a toy company to be named for such a vicious animal and changed it to 'Today's Kids.' Of course they're completely out of metal now. Today everything is plastic."

As for how the Pennant Winner was born, nobody seems to know. Obviously the inventor was both a baseball nut and a mechanical genius. Probably, in the grand tradition of industrial America, he was a lone tinkerer who brought his patent to Wolverine in about 1928. Just how skillfully the company realized that inventor's dream I was now reminded as Bill Lehren placed the game on my desk. It was a thing of beauty, its shiny metal field in perfect condition, without a dent or a scratch.

Lehren unwrapped the nine blue defensive players and put them in their slots. (The three base runners were red.) Then he unwrapped the ball and placed it against the pitching prong. I could still feel in my fingertips the fast and slow buttons that controlled that ball. I could also still feel the bat as I used to hold it back, waiting for the pitch, trying not to release it too soon or too late. Two fingers were best—one was too weak, three lacked finesse.

"Do you want to play a game?" Bill Lehren asked me. Of course I did. We took our positions on opposite sides of my desk and tried a few practice pitches and swings. But something was wrong—the ball rolled just a little unevenly. There was only one thing to do, and we both knew it. Bill took the game and lifted it down onto the rug.

The office where I write is in a commercial building on Lexington Avenue. I rent space along with other freelancers in fields such as advertising and fashion and graphic design. I've never closed my door, and I wasn't going to start now. Anyone who happened to pass my door that afternoon would have seen two men in their seventies, down on all fours—not an everyday spectacle in the American workplace.

Lehren batted first, and I positioned my fingers against the two pitching buttons. They felt instantly familiar. Bill said he was ready, and I fired a fast ball. The bat swung and the ball shot into the outfield and into the little slot beyond the center fielder marked HOME RUN. I tried a slow ball. Boom! Another home run. I tried to mix my pitches. They all came rocketing back: double, triple, home run. Finally a ball landed in the metal pocket in front of the left fielder with a satisfying PLONK. One out. But it was a disastrous start. The decades had left their residue of rust.

Then it was my turn to bat, and we switched ends. Holding the bat back, I felt as if my brain and my two fingertips were in perfect neurological rapport. Suddenly I heard the familiar click of the pitching prong being released and the equally familiar THOMP of the ball in the catcher's metal pocket. I hardly saw it go by. Priming myself for another fast pitch, I released the bat promptly and saw the ball dawdle toward the plate. The moment had lost none of its ignominy.

But then the old reflexes began to return, and we settled into a game that stayed close, obedient to the odds and probabilities of real baseball. Outside, the sun went down and the sky over Manhattan turned dark. We didn't notice; we were 12-year-old boys again, getting up and down from the rug every few minutes to change sides. Finally Bill said he had to catch his train back to the suburbs, and he packed up the game.

When we said good-bye at the elevator I had one last question for him: "Can you come back tomorrow?"

That article, called "Field of Tin," ran in the *Atlantic Monthly* in the summer of 2001, and, again, I heard from many readers, who found in my story an echo of some childhood memory of their own. Two letters in particular delighted me because they came from such an unexpected direction. I offer them here to remind you—again—of the gold you can strike if you tell ordinary stories and write out of your own humanity.

The first letter was from Ruth Armstrong, of Jonesville, Michigan, who said:

> I enjoyed your article about the "Field of Tin" baseball game, but even more, I am excited to see mention of a toy called "Sandy Andy" and your finding the company that made it.
>
> Every summer at the beach, in the 1930s when I was small, my little brother and I shared a new "Sandy Andy," along with our individually owned sand pails, shovels and tambourine-shaped sand strainers. When it was time to return home at the end of the summer, the scraped and rusting relics were reluctantly abandoned to promises of replacements the next year.
>
> So, years later, when I was making a set of tin beach toys for an article in *Nutshell News* (published in July 1993), I turned to the interloan library system to get a picture of my favorite toy, to no avail. I did get [a picture of] a sort of tin sand ferris wheel. But the toy that, to us, bore the name "Sandy Andy" was a little bucket elevator, with a hopper on an axle between the center posts that was counter-balanced by "Andy," a little tin figure of a man. When the hopper was full enough, down went the hopper to dump its load and up flew "Andy," then back

to level as the hopper lightened. It was red-and-yellow-and-blue painted tin and stood maybe 10 to 14 inches high. (*I* was smaller.)

After failing to find any picture to go by, I made my own little working model, about an inch and a quarter high, from memory. And I named it "Sandy Andy" in the article, but no one wrote to say they too had had one. It was fun, and I still wonder how close I came to copying the real toy. Since your friend Mr. Lehren knows all about the "Sandy Andy," could you ask him if a picture still exists? It would be so nice to solve one of *my* life's little mysteries. And, yes, the boys in my neighborhood had one of your baseball games, used mostly on the porch floor in hot summer.

I called Bill Lehren to pass along the request. He called back to say he couldn't find a picture of Sandy Andy anywhere, and I wrote Mrs. Armstrong to tell her the bad news. But four months later Bill wrote to say, "Lo and behold, I did stumble on something this morning, which I'll also send to Mrs. Armstrong." What he enclosed was a two-page spread from a Wolverine toy catalogue of about 1912. The left-hand page had a drawing of a contraption with a long incline that roughly resembled what I thought the toy would look like. The right-hand page described it:

Sandy Andy's busy little sand car hustling up and down the incline is wholly irresistable [*sic*] to any child. Simply put the sand into the hopper and Sandy Andy starts work as though the industries of the nation depended on its everlasting motion . . . It makes an ideal, realistic toy for the child—indoors in winter, outdoors in summer.

The lesson for writers in my correspondence with Mrs. Armstrong is that universal themes often come cloaked in unlikely garb. Not many people owned a mechanical baseball game; that's a highly specialized subject for a writer. But everyone had a favorite childhood toy or game, still vividly remembered. The fact that I had such a game, and that it was brought back to me at the other end of my life, can't help making a connection with readers who would like to hold *their* childhood toy one more time. They don't identify with my game as a baseball game. They identify with the *idea* of the game—a universal idea.

Moral: Write about things that are important to you, not about what you think readers will want to read, or editors will want to publish or agents will want to sell. Readers and editors and agents don't know what they want to read until they read it. If it's important to you, it will be important to other people.

This advice also applies to the occasional detour you may be tempted to make. In general I don't like writers to stray off the narrative trail; far too much writing is in organizational disarray. But sometimes an unforeseen jewel will pique your interest. Originally I had only intended to write about my baseball game as it related to my own life. But when I asked Bill Lehren about the history of Wolverine he told me about Benjamin Franklin Bain, and I was delighted to meet him: an American original, unknown to posterity.

I like to write about America, and I like my writing to be situated in a particular place. *Spring Training* is ostensibly a book about baseball; but the book is anchored in Bradenton, Florida. *Mitchell & Ruff* is ostensibly a profile of two jazz musicians; but the book is anchored in the small southern towns where Dwike Mitchell and Willie Ruff grew up and where their lives were crossed by people who taught them what they needed to know next. That's why I was so glad to hear about Benjamin Franklin Bain's tool-and-die shop in Pittsburgh. My mechanical baseball game wasn't born in a vacuum; somebody had to manufacture it, and Bain plugged my story into the larger story of industrial America and a factory that supplied America's kitchens with the utensils of domestic life. I gladly swerved from my narrative to tell the story of Wolverine and its subsequent move to Arkansas, where the advent of plastic put an end to the age of metal. Only that detour connected me to Mrs. Armstrong.

Ian Frazier, one of my favorite writers, is a prince of detours. Reading his long nonfiction pieces in the *New Yorker*, I've often found myself suddenly deflected down some bayou wholly unrelated to what has gone before, and I've thought, "How did we get *here?*" Frazier's *Family* is one of the most digressive of memoirs, and when I once interviewed him about that book I asked him about his inclination to wander. He said:

The artist Saul Steinberg once told me that I write fake boring books—books that you think would be boring, but then they're not. Faux boring. I tried to make this book sneakily interesting. I've always been willing to go in some off-the-wall direction—to drop everything and just run with it, where other writers might think, "I can't disrupt the fabric of my narrative." Ideally, each veer will make the narrative less boring.

That tendency of mine is a direct result of bouncing off William Shawn in the years when he was editor of *The New Yorker* and I was writing articles for him. It grew out of knowing what Shawn's threshold of boredom was. I would see his comments in the margins of my articles saying, "There's no reason for this part of the piece at all." Rick Hertzberg once wrote a wonderful profile of a guy who was a minor-league baseball owner. The guy goes to a bar and meets someone who says he has the biggest ranch in Texas. The guy doesn't believe him, and he takes him out to his ranch, which has millions of goats, and there's this long digression where everybody is driving around the prairie drunk in the middle of the morning. Shawn wrote in the margins, "This is neither funny nor interesting," and the section came out.

My objective in dealing with Shawn was to tease him into keeping a section like that—to get him to say, "Well, it's not funny or interesting, but O.K." I've often found, when people have read one of my pieces, that they will refer to something that was at first glance immaterial to the article. That was the one thing that stayed with them. Your objective is to find something that corresponds with the reader—something he or she has an affinity for, or can understand. It's a seduction. The reader thinks he knows what he wants, and if you can just tease him away from that he'll often have a better time than he would have had going where he thought he wanted to go.

In my article I seduced Mrs. Armstrong with Sandy Andy; that was her real interest. It was a lucky accident. How could I know that someone would read my piece who once owned the other Wolverine toy I mentioned? One of the pleasures of being a nonfiction writer is that you never know who you're reaching. I don't recommend Frazier's method as standard procedure for writers. On the contrary, I strongly recommend against it; if you pursue every whim you'll lose the necessary discipline of telling your story tightly. But dare to follow your interests if they call out to you strongly. You never know.

Which brings me to my other favorite response to my article. It was a letter from an artist named Lynne Perrella, and it was only three sentences long. But it enclosed a one-page excerpt from a book.

"Thank you for the remarkable story 'Field of Tin,'" Ms. Perrella wrote. "I have sent copies of the enclosed story about Pablo Neruda to a circle of friends, and now I will enjoy following up with a mailing of your story. Both, it seems to me, spring from a warm, familiar revisited place of creativity and humanity." The story that she enclosed was from a book called *The Gift*, by Lewis Hyde:

In an essay called "Childhood and Poetry," [the poet] Pablo Neruda once speculated on the origins of his work. Neruda was raised in Temuco, a frontier town in southern Chile. To be born in Temuco in 1904 must have been like being born in Oregon a hundred years ago. Rainy and mountainous, "Temuco was the farthest outpost in Chilean life in the southern territories," Neruda tells us. He remembers the main street as lined with hardware stores, which, since the local population couldn't read, hung out eye-catching signs: "an enormous saw, a giant cooking pot, a Cyclopean padlock, a mammoth spoon. Farther along the street, shoe stores— a colossal boot." Neruda's father worked on the railway. Their home, like others, had about it something of the air of a settlers' temporary camp: kegs of nails, tools and saddles lay about in unfinished rooms and under half-completed stairways.

Playing in the lot behind the house one day when he was still a little boy, Neruda discovered a hole in a fence board. "I looked through the hole and saw a landscape like the one behind our house, uncared for, and wild. I moved back a few steps, because I sensed vaguely that something was about to happen. All of a sudden a hand appeared—a tiny hand of a boy about my own age. By the time I came close again, the hand was gone, and in its place there was a marvelous white toy sheep.

"The sheep's wool was faded. Its wheels had escaped. All of this only made it more authentic. I had never seen such a wonderful sheep. I looked back through the hole, but the boy had disappeared. I went into the house and brought out a treasure of my own: a pine cone, opened, full of odor and resin, which I adored. I set it down in the same spot and went off with the sheep. I never saw either the hand or the boy again. And I have never seen a sheep like that either. The toy I lost finally in a fire. But even now, whenever I pass a toy shop, I look furtively into the window. It's no use. They don't make sheep like that anymore."

"This exchange of gifts—mysterious—settled deep inside me like a sedimentary deposit," Neruda once said. And he associates the exchange with his poetry. "I have been a lucky man. To feel the intimacy of brothers is a marvelous thing in life. To feel the love of people whom we love is a fire that feeds our life. But to feel the affection that comes from those whom we do not know, from those unknown to us, who are watching over our sleep and our solitude, over our dangers and our weaknesses— that is something still greater and more beautiful because it widens out the boundaries of our being, and unites all living things.

"That exchange brought home to me for the first time a precious idea: that all humanity is somehow together. It won't surprise you, then, that I have attempted to give something resiny, earthlike and fragrant in exchange for human brotherhood . . .

"This is the great lesson I learned in my childhood, in the back yard of a lonely house. Maybe it was nothing but a game two boys played who didn't know each other and wanted to pass to the other some good things of life. Yet maybe this small and mysterious exchange of gifts remained inside me also, deep and indestructible, giving my poetry light."

Lynne Perrella's letter to me struck me as a gift no less wonderful and mysterious. She saw a connection between a mechanical baseball game that a stranger brought to my Manhattan office in 2001 and an exchange of a toy sheep and a pine cone in a remote Chilean village in the early 1900s. But then I realized that of course the two stories are related—as all stories of shared humanity are related if we keep them simple and small. That realization was Ms. Perrella's real gift to me as a writer and as a teacher. Since then I've been sending her Neruda story to *my* circle of friends, just as she has been sending my article to hers.

POSTSCRIPT.

One Saturday afternoon in the fall of 2001, I went to a book-store in Rhinebeck, New York, to do a signing of my most recent book, *Easy to Remember: The Great American Song-writers and Their Songs*. I was also expected to give a short talk, and when I arrived I saw that about 25 chairs had been arranged in a semicircle for the hoped-for audience of book lovers.

As I was studying the room with the usual anxiety of authors wondering whether any book lovers will actually show up, I noticed a man and a woman hovering just beyond the chairs. I could see that they had something they very much wanted to tell me, but they were hesitant to intrude on my preoccupation with the logistics of the event.

To put them out of their misery I went over and introduced myself. The man said he had recently read my article in the *Atlantic Monthly* and realized that he had bought the same Wolverine game a few months earlier at a country antiques sale. He bought it because he thought it was a beautiful object, and he and his wife—their names were Jamie Saul and Marjorie Braman—were using it as a decoration in their weekend house. "When I saw in the paper that you were coming to Rhinebeck," Mr. Saul said, "we decided we wanted to give the game to you." They had already given me the gift of their faces wanting to tell me what they had in mind.

"Where *is* it?" I asked. They said it was in their car, which was parked outside. Could they bring it in? Did I have a way of taking it home? I said that my wife and I had come up from New York by train and could carry it back on the train.

Mr. Saul went out and came back with a large rectangular box, mottled with age and torn at the edges. The game was in its original box! It was duly pulled out and admired, along with the little cast-iron players and some long-ago box scores scrawled by some long-ago boy. Caroline, who had never seen the game she had heard so much about, protested that the gift was too generous. Mr. Saul dismissed her protest. "It means more to your husband than it does to me," he told her. So we slid the game back into the box and taped its edges shut with bookseller's tape, and I gave my talk, and we took the "Pennant Winner" back to New York.

The following summer I tried it out on my ten-year-old grandson, Mark Ferreira, a Little League outfielder. Mark is seldom without an electronic game in his palm, and I expected him to find Wolverine's metal contraptions klunky and archaic. But after two innings, as we were getting up from the floor to change ends, he said, "This is a fabulous game!"

13.

Change Is a Tonic

ONCE, IN THE MID-1980s, when Caroline and I were traveling in Morocco, we visited a friend of hers who lived in the medina—the old native quarter—of Marrakech. The friend was an American woman whom Caroline had known when they were both studying for a doctorate in anthropology; now she was doing fieldwork in Morocco. We arranged to meet her in the square outside the medina, and from there she took us to her house.

I had often walked as a tourist through the medinas of old Arab cities in North Africa like Fez and Tunis and had marveled at their intricacy as living and working communities. They were deeply mysterious—a labyrinth of narrow, noisy, crowded streets and alleys that branched off into other streets and alleys—and I often wondered what it was like to live there. What kind of homes were behind all those closed doors? Now I was about to see one of them.

We followed our friend into the dark center of Marrakech, trailing her around corners and past souks and market stalls that smelled of pungent foods and spices, snaking our way through a commotion of Arabs and Berbers and donkeys pulling carts—one of my favorite travel experiences—until she finally stopped at a door that didn't look any different from every other door.

Inside, she led us up some stairs to a large room that was quiet and light and airy. It seemed to be a gathering place for other Americans visiting or working in Morocco—a refuge from the surrounding clamor. One of them was a young woman who said she had come in for the day from the village where she lived. She was the classic American wholesome girl, blond and blue-eyed and fresh-faced.

We all sat around on pillows and ottomans and drank coffee and chatted. People came and went. The young woman kept looking at me. "Didn't I know you at Yale?" she asked. I said I didn't think so; she wasn't in Branford College or in any of my writing classes.

"I know we've met," she said. I asked her when she graduated. She said she was in the class of 1984. I had left Yale in 1979; we couldn't have overlapped, even when she was a freshman. But she continued to look at me.

Finally she said, "Did you ever come back to Yale to talk at a conference on alternative careers?"

A dim light bulb went on in my brain. One snowy Saturday in midwinter, after I had been back in New York for a year or two, I took a train to New Haven. Yale was holding a conference for students who didn't want to go into law or medicine or business or banking or consulting or any of the other mainstream professions. Those fields had always sent recruiters to college campuses. But nobody recruited for all the alternative ways of making a life. Somebody at Yale remembered me as Mr. Alternative, and I was asked back.

I told the young woman in Marrakech that I did indeed come from New York to talk at a conference on alternative careers. I could still picture the scene: a ragged circle of young men and women sitting on the floor, looking up at me for news of the larger world where they would soon have to figure out what to do.

"I knew it!" the young woman said. "You changed my life."

That sentence always carries a flicker of dread. "You told me something once," a former student will say to a former teacher, and the teacher's first thought is, "OhmyGod, I hope I didn't give her bum advice."

"Because of what you told us that day," the young woman went on, "I completely changed how I thought about what to do with my life, and that's why I'm here."

"What are you doing?" I asked.

"After I graduated from Yale I joined the Peace Corps," she said, "and now I'm working in a Berber village out in the desert, about fifty miles from here."

But I still had one all-important question: "Do you like it?"

"I love it," she said.

What did I tell those alternative seekers at Yale? Mainly I told them the story of my own alternative life: how I period-ically uprooted myself and how I never did—or continued to do—what I was expected to do. I didn't go into the family business; I didn't stay at the *Herald Tribune*; I didn't stay in New York; I didn't stay at Yale, and I didn't stay at the Book-of-the-Month Club. I always left when the work ceased to be fulfilling. I urged the Yale students not to become the prisoner of expectations that were not the right ones for them—other people's expectations. I saluted my father for not holding me to *his* expectations for me.

A few years later, in 1988, I made the same points in a commencement talk at Wesleyan University, and I still hear from people who were there. Whenever I talk to graduating seniors I'm mindful that I also have a captive audience of parents and grandparents, uncles and aunts, teachers and coaches—all the elders whose love and support have brought the graduates to this long-awaited day. I use the occasion to remind them that their children have one life and should be allowed to follow their own best dreams.

Don't assume [I told the Wesleyan seniors] that if you don't do what other people seem to be insisting that you do, it's the end of the world. As my experience with my father proves, something very nourishing can happen—a blessing, a form of grace. Be ready to be surprised by grace. And be wary of security as a goal. It may often look like life's best prize. Usually it's not . . .

One of the themes I've been talking to you about this morning—though I haven't used the word—is separation. It's very much on your mind today, and it will be many times again, and it will always be painful; none of the changes I made in my life were anything but scary at the time I made them. But there are two ways to think about separation: as a loss, or as a beginning. To separate is to start fresh.

For you, I hope today will be the first of many separations that will mean putting behind you something you've done well and beginning something you'll do just as well, or better. Keep separating yourself from any project that's not up to your highest standards of what's right for you—and for the broader community where you can affect the quality of life: your home, your town, your children's schools, your state, your country, your world. Live usefully; nothing in your life will be as satisfying as making a difference in somebody else's life.

Separate yourself from cynics and from peddlers of despair. Don't let anyone tell you it won't work.

After my talk, three professors in cap and gown sought me out. One of them, presumably also speaking for the other two, said, "That does it—I'm getting out of this dead-ass job." Wesleyan sent my talk to all its alumni, and I began to get letters from them. They said I had given them the push they needed to get out of careers that had gone stale. Some of the changes they told me about were dramatic, involving high risk. Ten years later the class of 1988 invited me to their tenth reunion; they wanted a recharge.

It comes down to permission. I'm struck by how scarce that commodity is. I go around America giving people permission to be who they want to be, and I think: Why me? How did *I* get stuck with this job? Isn't that what our schools are supposed to be doing? The answer, I've discovered, is that most Americans look back on their education as a permission-denying experience—a long, winding trail of don'ts and can'ts and shouldn'ts. I've made that statement in talks to college presidents and professors and school principals and headmasters, and not one of them has ever stood up and said, "How dare you say such a terrible thing?"

The reason, probably, is that all of them remember the restraints and prohibitions that were put in the path of their own advancement: the niggling caveats of dissertation committees, the ungenerous barbs of peer reviewers, the grim warnings that they will perish unless they keep publishing books they don't want to write and nobody needs to read. When I mention "permission," the word detonates like a bomb; I've mentioned the unmentionable. I suspect that it would be just as threatening to a roomful of CEOs and middle managers: no alternative thinkers wanted.

Yet what any good executive should be looking for is general intelligence, breadth, originality, imagination, audacity, a sense of history, a sense of cultural context, a sense of humor, a sense of wonder—not just someone to fill a specific job. America has more than enough people willing to go through life being someone else's precise fit. What we need are men and women who will break the mold of conventional thinking, who won't buy the phrase "We've always done it this way. This way is good enough."

Those qualities also go into good writing. Bad writing is tired and predictable; nobody wants a cautious writer. When you write, call on the best of your character. And make sure you're living the life you want to live.

My journey ends with one more change of direction I gave myself permission to make. I've played the piano all my life, but I had never played in public. When I crossed over into the Medicare years I decided to see if I could become a musician.

I had the good luck to be born with a good ear, and I had the further good luck to have a piano teacher wise enough to bend to my perversities. Her name was Editha Messer, and I was about ten when she started coming to our house to give me lessons. She plied me with the usual fare of early keyboard instruction: the dreary exercises of Hanon, the simple tunes of the Diller-Quaile songbook, the pedagogical chestnuts like Edward MacDowell's "To a Wild Rose."

I hated having to learn and memorize those songs. Something in me also didn't want to learn to read music. But I liked the contours of the melodies and the colors of the harmonies, and I would try to fake my way by ear to the notes I was supposed to be reading. Mrs. Messer wasn't fooled. She stuck to the canons of her trade, and we labored on, week after week, making little progress and not having any fun: teacher and student yoked in a forced march to nowhere. I would be impaled forever on MacDowell's wild rose.

One day Mrs. Messer stopped the lesson and said, "You're never going to learn to read music"—she knew her pupil well—"but you have a good ear, so I'm going to teach you the chords. If you know harmony you'll be able to play any song you hear." She took out a little brown notebook that I can still visualize and wrote out C-E-G and the other major and minor chords. Then she showed me what the chords looked like, and what they sounded like, and how they functioned within the key of C, and how they were all related in an elegant mathematical system. A universe I never knew existed was revealed to me that afternoon.

With that body of information Editha Messer gave me the tools I needed to become my own teacher. She freed me to go where I wanted to go, just as Dean Root would later free me to get on with my life by waiving the credits I needed to graduate from Princeton. Both of them were alternative thinkers. Mrs. Messer had the largeness of heart to throw away the rules of how piano teachers are expected to teach. Instead she asked herself: what does my student want to learn?

I started by learning to play hymns—a crash course in harmony because hymns require a chord with almost every melody note. Then I inherited from my sister Nancy a jazz teacher from the Bronx named Joseph Kruger. It was Joe Kruger's messianic mission to teach boys and girls—even talentless boys and girls—how to play the popular songs of the day enjoyably and without fear. Under his system, which he called a swing bass, the left hand moved in a tireless shuttle, enabling his pupils to render current hits like "Stormy Weather" with a steady rhythmical bounce. (I can still hear Nancy's peppy "Paper Moon.") Hymns ebbed out of my repertory and jazz slipped in.

Meanwhile I had begun my lifelong love affair with the great American songbook—the thousands of songs written for Broadway musicals and Hollywood movies during the

40-year golden age that started with *Show Boat*. From an early age I remember my parents bringing home the sheet music from Broadway musicals like Cole Porter's *Anything Goes*. Later they took me to the actual shows, and then I began seeing them on my own. After the war, when my job at the *Herald Tribune* gave me two tickets to every opening night, I saw *Guys and Dolls*, *South Pacific*, *West Side Story*, *My Fair Lady* and dozens of other great and not-so-great musicals. All those songs went into my ear and into my brain, where, to this day, they are computerized for instant recall, along with countless movie songs, popular standards and songs from earlier musicals, which I learned by listening to LP records that reconstructed those bygone scores. In 2001, I put my knowledge of those composers and lyricists into the book *Easy to Remember*. That book and my other book about music and musicians, *Mitchell & Ruff*, are my two favorites and the ones I most enjoyed writing.

At the piano, my chords at first were no more than serviceable—the plain triads of elementary harmony. That changed when I went to college and heard a senior named Bus Davis play the songs he had written for Princeton Triangle Club shows. (Later, as Buster Davis, he was a longtime Broadway vocal director.) What I heard coming out of Bus Davis's piano were harmonies I had never imagined—a style I came to think of as the New York sound, infinitely sophisticated, suggestive of chic nightclubs and cabarets and dancing till dawn at the Rainbow Room. Bobby Short is an example of the many jazz pianists who have made it their signature.

Bus Davis's piano touched an emotional nerve I didn't know

I had. Those chords were also waiting for me—for *me!*—somewhere in the 88 keys. But where were they? I was determined to find them. By watching Bus and analyzing his chords I saw that they weren't freaks from out of the blue. They were variants of the conventional "correct" chord. They were created by adding notes to give the chord a jazz color and by subtracting the notes that made the chord uninteresting. C-E-G, for instance, is the fundamental chord in Western music. But no good jazz pianist would play it; it's too boring. It would get changed, in the right hand, to B-D-G. The D replaces the E, thereby removing one of the notes in the boring triad, and the C is replaced by B. That B, known as a major seventh, gives the chord its jazz kick and is the identifying anchor of the style. But the chord still sounds like a C chord because it's grounded in the left hand by some combination of C and E and G— often a C-E tenth. The roots of the chord are still intact.

That B—that major seventh—radicalized me. Since then I've never played C-E-G, except when I play nursery songs for my grandchildren, and even then the B tends to sneak in. (I know: C-E-G is Mozart's chord, and Beethoven's chord. But the truth is, I don't much like Mozart; my guys are Rachmaninoff and Ravel.) Starting from that discovery, I began to find variants for all the standard chords: to create my own unified vocabulary. I also looked around for models to emulate. The one I fixated on was the Manhattan cocktail pianist Cy Walter. His style was the height of urbanity, and I spent many hours watching him play and listening to his records, trying to figure out how he did what he did. By the time I left Princeton to go into the army I had the harmonies I wanted.

In the army that style gave me three or four of the best friends I ever had. Because I missed having a piano to play, I would gravitate to any piano I found in a USO club and would coddle myself with show tunes. The New York sound, it turned out, acted as a magnet. In that vast sea of undifferentiated enlisted men it would catch the ear of the one soldier who had grown up in Indianapolis or Rochester or St. Paul reading the *New Yorker* and dreaming of the larger world. What brought us together was a shared language of music. But that was only the beginning of all the interests we found we had in common.

After the war I took up my life as a journalist and husband and father and only played the piano as a hobby. Then, one day, at Yale, I heard the jazz pianist Dwike Mitchell playing with Willie Ruff, his partner in the Mitchell-Ruff Duo. It was another Bus Davis moment. All of us recognize our teacher when he or she comes along: the person who can take us where we want to go next. Mitchell's style and sensibility were my style and sensibility, raised to a high mathematical power. Suddenly it dawned on me that I wasn't playing any better in my fifties than I had played in my early twenties. That didn't seem right, and when I moved back to New York I asked Mitchell if I could study with him. For the next 20 years I went to his apartment almost every Saturday morning.

Like Editha Messer, my new teacher built on what he was given; he didn't try to turn me into a copy of himself. His chords moved me with their complexity and their high emotional content, and gradually I learned most of them. Emotion, to Mitchell, is everything. When he plays a Gershwin song he isn't, strictly, playing Gershwin's song. He's playing how he feels about the song at that moment, depending on a whole set of variables: his mood, his health, what's happening in his life, whether it's raining outside. I've never heard him play a song the same way twice.

"If you feel a certain emotion while you're playing the piano," he kept assuring me, "your listeners will feel it, too." I found that hard to believe; I guess I thought I had to somehow seize the listener's attention. But I took what he said on faith—it's the same advice I give to writers—and gradually I learned to trust my emotions. Mitchell moved away from chords and began to focus on touch—he quieted me down—and on phrasing. He taught me to sing as a jazz singer sings, phrasing the lyrics as they would be phrased in conversation, not as they are printed on the sheet music, tethered to each melody note.

Those singing lessons carried over to the piano. I now try to phrase every song with its lyric in mind—to play Hart more than Rodgers, Ira Gershwin more than George—because the songs first engage us with the story they tell: "It was just one of those things," "Somewhere over the rainbow," "I left my heart in San Francisco." I also discovered how powerful the songs are in their associations: an instant mechanism for recovering the past. "Pat and I first danced to that song," people tell me, or "That song takes me back to Naples during the war." I could see their faces change, their pains and disappointments drop away. I realized that a pianist who plays these American *lieder* ends up doing more than he signed up to do.

When I was in my late sixties, some of my friends began to urge me to play in public. "Your music gives people pleasure," they said, and I liked that idea; if you can do something that gives people pleasure, you ought to do it. But the idea also made me uncomfortable; WASPs are told not to make a display of themselves. It was O.K. for me to give lectures about writing; that was an extension of my writer's persona, a role long approved by society and raised to a bravura art form by Charles Dickens and Mark Twain. But to perform! What if someone I knew saw me playing the piano in a restaurant or a bar? I wasn't ready for that. When people asked me if I played the piano I would say "a little" or "not really." Which wasn't true. I was guilty of the tribal sin I most despised: false apologizing.

That had to stop. "If you want to be a professional musician, then act like a professional musician," I told myself. I forced myself out and got some gigs at the Cornelia Street Cafe, in Greenwich Village, and at book parties and art openings. I was still very self-conscious. The hard part wasn't the playing; I wasn't nervous about possibly hitting the wrong notes. The hard part was breaking the reticence barrier. But every time I played I learned something about performing that I couldn't have learned in any other way, and it was easier the next time.

I cast around for other musicians to play with—I wanted to know how to play with other instruments—and fate delivered me to Arnold Roth. A well-known cartoonist and illustrator, Arnie was from an Orthodox family of five brothers who were told at an early age to learn a skill that would help support the family. He learned the saxophone and has moonlighted as a musician ever since, leading dance bands and playing in small combos. Musically, he and I made a good team; we both had a warm sound and we knew a million songs. In experience, however, I was coming from the opposite end of life's arc, and I did some residual apologizing.

One day Arnie said, "I've made it a point never to be embarrassed. You and I know there are certain days when we're not playing as well as on other days, but we're playing better than anyone in the room can play." It was the perfect thing to tell me, and it cured me of my waffling. Arnie and I are now in our second decade of playing regularly together. People tell us that our music gives them pleasure, and I've even begun to let myself believe it.

I needn't have worried that I would be recognized by someone I knew when we played a commercial gig. Musicians, I found, are an invisible class of providers, like waiters and caterers and bartenders, unnoticed as individual men and women. One night Arnie and I played at a birthday party in one of New York's haughtiest private clubs. The dinner was preceded by a long cocktail hour, and several of the guests happened to be people I knew quite well. None of them noticed me. That's when I knew I had become a musician. I also felt liberated from an old oppression. I'm not a fan of cocktail parties—the endless standing and the mindless talking. As a paid pianist I had stumbled on the ultimate trifecta: I was doing something I loved to do, I got to sit down, and I didn't have to talk to anyone.

I also learned about the solidarity of labor. Arnie and I were once hired to play a wedding rehearsal dinner at a country club in Connecticut. During the cocktail hour, waitresses circulated among us passing trays of hors d'oeuvres, and I assumed that we would also be offered an occasional canapé to fortify us through the evening. We weren't. Around eight o'clock, when it was time for our break, I asked Arnie what we were going to do about dinner. His face said no problem; why do you even ask?

"What we do," he said, "is we go to the kitchen." He put down his sax and led me unerringly through the crowd, guided by some musician's radar born of many long nights on the bandstand, to an unmarked swinging door. Inside the door we found three women feverishly slicing and dicing and tending to a multitude of pots and pans. I was struck by how hard they were working. They welcomed us as fellow drudges, sat us down at a kitchen table and brought us dinner on two plates. I was in the American workforce!

One big bonus of my new career has been the chance to work with professional musicians. They are unfailingly generous men and women, totally committed to their art. That's something I'm glad I lived long enough to find out. Old age hasn't turned out to be a closing door; I've made far more friends in the past ten years—through music—than in any other decade of my life. Many of them are people who come to hear me play. Some are piano students—people who want to learn the chords I once wanted to learn. Some are singers and arrangers who worked with me on a musical revue I wrote about a summer community, "What's the Point?" which had an off-Broadway run in June 2003, the summer of my 80th year.

Through it all I've discovered that the piano player's life has one unchanging hazard: the piano. There will always be something wrong with the piano, but I never know what form the wrongness will take. It will be out of tune. Some keys will be stuck. The pedal will be broken. No bench or chair will be provided. I was once hired to play at a wedding reception in an arts club in New York. The mother of the bride and I had spoken several times about the logistics of the event: hours, pay, type of music, where the piano would be placed. Everything was set. A week before the wedding I thought, "I'd just better make sure that arts club *has* a piano." I called the mother and put the question to her. There was a small intake of breath. "I never thought about that," she said. "Now that you mention it, I don't think the club does have a piano." I assured her that a piano could be rented. I explained that there are good pianos and bad pianos, and I gave her the name of a woman who could rent her a good one. When the wedding day arrived and I reported for duty I was led to an instrument that looked like a factory reject. The mother of the bride had left a note for me, written in her best hand on her best engraved stationery: DEAR MR. ZINSSER. SORRY ABOUT THE PIANO.

I now arrive early at every job to assess the damage and try some minor repairs. I'm most depressed when the "hold" pedal is broken—the pedal that sustains the notes. The result is a brittle staccato in the right hand that negates the legato sound that my style depends on. At such moments I remember the words of my teacher, Dwike Mitchell, who, in a lifetime of playing concerts, has been confronted by more than his allotted share of lemons.

"I learned long ago," he told me, "that it does no good to complain. Once you start complaining you're throwing yourself into another state. You think, 'This damn piano,' and you get mad at it, and when you get angry you play angry, and you can't project who *you* really are because you've been transformed into an angry person and you have all kinds of things going through your mind. Instead you say, 'What *does* it do? Will it do *any*thing? Let's check it out.' You try to work with it, and sometimes it's a lot of fun because many pianos give you a different response from the one you're used to, and that makes you play differently." Once I heard Mitchell play in a concert hall whose new piano had one note near middle C that he couldn't stand. His solution was to voice every chord differently throughout the concert to avoid the offending note.

That intellectual feat came back to me when I was faced with my first broken pedal on one of my first jobs. I was angry and upset, and I treated my wounds with a few minutes of self-pity. Finally I got around to asking myself, "What *does* it do?" I found that if I played mostly in the lower register I could carry the melody with chords and could hold those chords down myself, thereby avoiding the tinny upper notes. It was a long and difficult night, but it got me over my fear of broken pedals.

Much of what Dwike Mitchell taught me about playing the piano has nothing to do with music. It has to do with conduct and character. When I sometimes feel a twinge of disappointment if the crowd at one of my gigs is smaller than I expected, I hear Mitchell saying, "It's a privilege to play for one other person." That credo has helped me through many thin situations, both as a public pianist and as a public speaker. I've stopped worrying about conditions that I can't control or change. I just do what I came to do, as well as I can.

That's also all you can do as a writer. When you write about your life, stop worrying about editors and publishers and agents and about all the readers you hope to reach. It's a privilege to write for one other person. Do it with gratitude and with pleasure.